Sustainable Global Outsourcing

Technology, Work and Globalization

The *Technology, Work and Globalization* series was developed to provide policy makers, workers, managers, academics and students with a deeper understanding of the complex interlinks and influences between technological developments, including information and communication technologies, work organizations and patterns of globalization. The mission of the series is to disseminate rich knowledge based on deep research about relevant issues surrounding the globalization of work that is spawned by technology.

Also in the series:

Sustainable Global Outsourcing

Achieving Social and Environmental Responsibility in Global IT and Business Process Outsourcing

Ron Babin
Ryerson University, Canada

and

Brian Nicholson
Manchester Business School, UK

First published 2012 by
PALGRAVE MACMILLAN

Palgrave Macmillan in the UK is an imprint of Macmillan Publishers Limited,
registered in England, company number 785998, of Houndmills, Basingstoke,
Hampshire RG21 6XS.

Palgrave Macmillan in the US is a division of St Martin's Press LLC,
175 Fifth Avenue, New York, NY 10010.

Palgrave Macmillan is the global academic imprint of the above companies
and has companies and representatives throughout the world.

Palgrave® and Macmillan® are registered trademarks in the United States,
the United Kingdom, Europe and other countries.

ISBN 978–0–230–28507–1

This book is printed on paper suitable for recycling and made from fully
managed and sustained forest sources. Logging, pulping and manufacturing
processes are expected to conform to the environmental regulations of the
country of origin.

A catalogue record for this book is available from the British Library.

Library of Congress Cataloging-in-Publication Data
Babin, Ronald P.
    Sustainable global outsourcing : achieving social and environmental
    responsibility in global IT and business process outsourcing / by
    Ron Babin, Brian Nicholson.
       p.   cm.
    ISBN 978–0–230–28507–1
    1. Computer software industry—Subcontracting.   2. Computer
    software—Development—Management.   3. Information technology—
    Management.   4. Sustainable development.   5. Globalization—
    Economic aspects.   I. Nicholson, Brian, 1967–   II. Title.
    HD9696.63.A2B33 2012
    658.4′058—dc23   2012024027

10   9   8   7   6   5   4   3   2   1
21 20 19 18 17 16 15 14 13 12

Printed and bound in Great Britain by
CPI Antony Rowe, Chippenham and Eastbourne

Contents

Figures

Tables

Series Editors' Preface

We launched this series in 2006 to provide policy makers, workers, managers, academics and students with a deeper understanding of the complex interlinks and influences among technological developments, including in information and communication technologies (ICT), work, organizations and globalization. We have always felt that technology is all too often positioned as the welcome driver of globalization. The popular press neatly packages technology's influence on globalization with snappy sound bites, such as: "Any work that can be digitized will be globally sourced." Most glossy cover stories assume that all globalization is progressive, seamless and intractable, and that it leads to unmitigated good. But what we are experiencing in the twenty-first century in terms of the interrelationships between technology, work and globalization is both profound and highly complex.

The mission of this series is to disseminate rich knowledge based on deep research about relevant issues surrounding the globalization of work that is spawned by technology. To us, substantial research on globalization considers multiple perspectives and levels of analyses. We seek to publish research based on in-depth study of developments in technology, work and globalization and their impacts on and relationships with individuals, organizations, industries and countries. We welcome perspectives from business, economics, sociology, public policy, cultural studies, law and other disciplines that contemplate both larger trends and micro-developments from Asian, African, Australian and Latin American, as well as from North American and European, viewpoints.

As of this writing, we have 16 books published or under contract. These books are introduced below.

1) *Global Sourcing of Business and IT Services*, by Leslie P. Willcocks and Mary C. Lacity, is the first book in the series. The book is based on over 1,000 interviews with clients, providers and advisers, and 15 years of study. The specific focus is on developments in outsourcing, offshoring and mixed sourcing practices from client and provider perspectives in a globalizing world. The authors found many organizations struggling. They also found some organizations adeptly creating global sourcing networks that are agile, effective and cost-efficient. But they did so

only after a tremendous amount of trial and error and close attention to details. All our participant organizations acted in a context of fast-moving technology, rapid development of supply-side offerings and ever-changing economic conditions.

2) *Knowledge Processes in Globally Distributed Contexts*, by Julia Kotlarsky, Ilan Oshri and Paul van Fenema, examines the management of knowledge processes of global knowledge workers. Based on substantial case studies and interviews, the authors – along with their network of co-authors – provide frameworks, practices and tools that consider how to develop, coordinate and manage knowledge processes in order to create synergetic value in globally distributed contexts. Chapters address knowledge-sharing, social ties, transactive memory, imperative learning, work division and many other social and organizational practices to ensure successful collaboration in globally distributed teams.

3) *Offshore Outsourcing of IT Work*, by Mary C. Lacity and Joseph W. Rottman, explores the practices for successfully outsourcing IT work from Western clients to offshore providers. Based on over 200 interviews with 26 Western clients and their offshore providers in India, China and Canada, the book details client-side roles of chief information officers, program management officers and project managers and identifies project characteristics that differentiate successful from unsuccessful projects. The authors examine ten engagement models for moving IT work offshore and describe proven practices to ensure that offshore outsourcing is successful for both client and provider organizations.

4) *Exploring Virtuality within and beyond Organizations*, by Niki Panteli and Mike Chiasson, argues that there has been a limited conceptualization of virtuality and its implications for the management of organizations. Based on illustrative cases, empirical studies and theorizing on virtuality, this book goes beyond the simple comparison between the virtual and the traditional to explore the different types, dimensions and perspectives of virtuality. Almost all organizations are virtual, but they differ theoretically and substantively in their virtuality. By exploring and understanding these differences, researchers and practitioners gain a deeper understanding of the past, present and future possibilities of virtuality. The collection is designed to be indicative of current thinking and approaches, and it provides a rich basis for further research and reflection in this important area of management and information systems research and practice.

5) *ICT and Innovation in the Public Sector*, by Francesco Contini and Giovan
   Francesco Lanzara, examines the theoretical and practical issues related
   to implementing innovative ICT solutions in the public sector. The
   book is based on a major research project sponsored and funded by
   the Italian government (Ministry of University and Research) and
   coordinated by Italy's National Research Council and the University
   of Bologna during the years 2002–2006. The authors, along with a
   number of co-authors, explore the complex interplay between technology and institutions, drawing on multiple theoretical traditions
   such as institutional analysis, actor network theory, social systems theory, organization theory and transaction costs economics. Detailed
   case studies offer realistic and rich lessons. These case studies include
   e-justice in Italy and Finland, e-bureaucracy in Austria and Money
   Claim On-Line in England and Wales.

6) *Outsourcing Global Services: Knowledge, Innovation, and Social Capital*,
   edited by Ilan Oshri, Julia Kotlarsky and Leslie P. Willcocks, assembles
   the best work from the active participants in the *Information Systems
   Workshop on Global Sourcing* which began in 2007 in Val d'Isere, France.
   Because the quality of the contributions was exceptional, we invited
   the program chairs to edit a book based on the best papers at the conference. The collection provides in-depth insights into the practices
   that lead to success in outsourcing global services. Written by internationally acclaimed academics, it covers best practices in IT outsourcing,
   business process outsourcing and netsourcing.

7) *Global Challenges for Identity Policies*, by Edgar Whitley and Ian Hosein,
   provides a perfect fit for the series in that the authors examine identity policies for modern societies in terms of the political, technical
   and managerial issues needed to prevent identity fraud and theft. The
   scale of the problem exceeds political boundaries, and the authors
   cover national identity policies in Europe and the rest of the world.
   Much of the book provides in-depth discussion and analysis of the
   United Kingdom's National Identity Scheme. The authors provide
   recommendations for identity and technical policies.

8) *E-Governance for Development*, by Shirin Madon, examines the rapid
   proliferation of e-governance projects aimed at introducing ICT to
   improve systems of governance and thereby to promote development.
   In this book, the author unpacks the theoretical concepts of development and governance in order to propose an alternative conceptual
   framework, which encourages a deeper understanding of macro- and
   micro-level political, social and administrative processes within which

e-governance projects are implemented. The book draws on more than 15 years of research in India during which time many changes have occurred in terms of the country's development ideology, governance reform strategy and ICT deployment.

9) *Bricolage, Care and Information*, edited by Chrisanthi Avgerou, Giovan Francesco Lanzara and Leslie P. Willcocks, celebrates Claudio Ciborra's *Legacy in Information Systems Research*. Claudio Ciborra was one of the most innovative thinkers in the field of information systems. He was one of the first scholars who introduced institutional economics in the study of Information Systems; he elaborated new concepts, such as "the platform organization" and "formative contexts"; and he contributed to the development of a new perspective altogether through Heideggerian phenomenology. This book contains the most seminal work of Claudio Ciborra and the work of other authors who were inspired by his work and built upon it.

10) *China's Emerging Outsourcing Capabilities*, edited by Mary C. Lacity, Leslie P. Willcocks and Yingqin Zheng, marks the tenth book in the series. The Chinese government has assigned a high priority to science and technology as its future growth sectors. China has a national plan to expand the information technology outsourcing (ITO) and business process outsourcing (BPO) sectors. Beyond the hopes of its leaders, is China ready to compete in the global ITO and BPO markets? Western companies are becoming more interested in extending their global network of ITO and BPO services beyond India, and they wish to learn more about China's ITO and BPO capabilities. In this book, we accumulate the findings of the best research on China's ITO and BPO sector by the top scholars in the field of information systems.

11) *The Outsourcing Enterprise: From Cost Management to Collaborative Innovation* is by Leslie Willcocks, Sara Cullen and Andrew Craig. The central question answered in this book is: "How does an organization leverage the ever growing external services market to gain operational, business and strategic advantage?" The book covers the foundations of mature outsourcing enterprises that have moved outsourcing to the strategic agenda by building the relationship advantage, selecting and levering suppliers, keeping control through core retained capabilities and collaborating to innovate. The book provides proven practices used by mature outsourcing enterprises to govern, design and measure outsourcing. The final chapter presents practices on how mature outsourcing enterprises can prepare for the next generation of outsourcing.

12) *Governing through Technology: Information Nets and Social Practice*, by Jannis Kallinikos, is thoughtful scholarship that examines the relationships among information, technology and social practices. The author discusses the regulative regime of technology and issues of human agency control and complexity in a connected world. He provides a valuable counter-perspective to show that social practices are, in part, unmistakably products of technologies; that technologies are, through historical processes, embedded in the social fabric; and that, even if the idea of technological determinism is naive, the notion of the regulative regime of technology remains alive and well into the internet age.

13) *Enterprise Mobility: Tiny Technology with Global Impact on Information Work*, by Carsten Sørensen, explores how mobile technologies are radically changing the way work is done in organizations. The author defines enterprise mobility as the deployment of mobile information technology for organizational purposes. The author contrasts how large technology projects in organizations, such as enterprise resource planning (ERP) implementations, will increasingly be managed differently because of mobile technology. The introduction of mobile technology supporting organizational information work will often be driven by individuals, small teams or as part of departmental facilitation of general communication services.

14) *Collaboration in Outsourcing: A Journey to Quality*, edited by Sjaak Brinkkemper and Slinger Jansen, is based on an integrated program of outsourcing research at Utrecht University in the Netherlands. The book is written for practitioners and is based on interviews and case studies in many global outsourcing firms, including Cisco, IBM, Deloitte, Infosys, Logica and Patni – to name a few. The 16 chapters are short, tight and written to communicate best practices quickly. The chapters cover the topics of governance, knowledge management relationship management and new trends in software development outsourcing.

15) *Advanced Outsourcing Practice: Rethinking ITO, BPO, and Cloud Services*, by Mary Lacity and Leslie Willcocks, is written for seasoned outsourcing practitioners who are ready to master the advanced practices. In particular, the authors show how practitioners can optimize the strategic value inherent in offshore outsourcing shared services, bundled services, impact outsourcing, advanced BPO, rural outsourcing and cloud computing. This book will be a vital resource for all practitioners looking to reinvigorate, leverage and render strategic their outsourcing enterprise.

16) *Sustainable Global Outsourcing: Achieving Social and Environmental Responsibility*, by Ron Babin and Brian Nicholson, examines how clients and providers achieve social and environmental sustainability in outsourcing relationships. The book covers the reasons to consider sustainability and the ways in which sustainability can be measured and integrated to deliver shared benefits. The book includes case studies, survey results and frameworks that effectively illustrate lessons and arm practitioners with actionable insights.

In addition to the books already published and under contract, we have several other manuscripts under review but always need more. We encourage other researchers to submit proposals to the series, as we envision a protracted need for scholars to deeply and richly analyze and conceptualize the complex relationships among technology, work and globalization. Please follow the submissions guidelines on the Palgrave Macmillan website (www.palgrave-usa.com/Info/Submissions.aspx).

Leslie P. Willcocks
Mary C. Lacity
January 2012

Acknowledgments

The authors would like to thank several organizations and individuals for their contributions to the research on which this book is based.

First we thank the executives at Rio Tinto, Enbridge, Accenture and Tata Consultancy Services in Toronto, Canada, and Montreal, Canada, who contributed their time and ideas to this research. Second the executives at Accenture in Bangalore, India, and at a large Indian outsourcing firm were gracious and informative in their discussion of corporate social responsibility (CSR) in outsourcing. Finally the executives at Co-operative Financial Services in Manchester, UK, particularly Steve Briggs and Jim Slack, along with Graham Greene and several executives from Steria, the outsourcing service provider to the co-op, were very helpful and supportive as we developed our concepts.

The Manchester Business School at the University of Manchester, UK, and the Centre for Development Informatics there were supportive and helpful in the development of this manuscript. The Ted Rogers School of Management at Ryerson University in Toronto, Canada, encouraged Ron as a doctoral student while he developed his thesis and this manuscript over the last four years.

Our colleagues in outsourcing research meet annually at the Global Sourcing Workshop (GSW). Our research benefited tremendously from the encouragement and insight of fellow researchers and practitioners at the GSW sessions in Blackstone, Colorado, USA; Zermatt, Switzerland; and Courchevel, France, where we presented key concepts of this research. We say thank you in particular to Ilan Oshri, Julia Kotlarsky, Mary Lacity and Leslie Willcocks. They helped shed light to grow our ideas in the early stages. Mary and Leslie were especially supportive as we wrote this book.

Three outsourcing professional organizations were immensely helpful in this research. First the Centre for Outsourcing Research and Education (CORE), Toronto, Canada, allowed Ron to collect data, develop concepts and present the results in seminars and professional education sessions. Second the CSR sub-committee of the International Association of Outsourcing Professionals (IAOP) provided a group of like-minded individuals, including Scott Phillips, Bill Hefley and Pam O'Dell; collectively we believe that CSR and sustainability in outsourcing will make the world a better place. Third the National Outsourcing Association (NOA) helped to publicize our concepts with a workshop in Manchester, UK, for which we thank our friend Adrian Quayle.

Finally our family and friends curiously asked us what we were working on late at night and early in the morning, on weekends and when others were usually resting. Hopefully this book will explain some of our passion for writing and talking about CSR and sustainability. We each owe a debt of gratitude to our spouses and children. To Susanne, Emily and India, to Wendy, David and Kaitlyn, thank you for your patience and understanding.

This book is the beginning of an important trend that affects all who participate in outsourcing. We expect further developments and research as awareness of the need for sustainable outsourcing grows. We invite you to stay in touch with us and to continue the discussion at sustainableoutsourcing.com. We hope you will enjoy our first book on sustainable global outsourcing.

Ron Babin
Brian Nicholson

Foreword

It is impossible today not to be highly conscious of a growing political, business and social focus on so-called compassionate capitalism. The multitude of threads which contribute to this agenda can be seen in US Presidential elections, the continuing debates about bankers' bonuses and in the ever-growing list of organizations that now have ethical policies, programs, products and services. It seems that change is in the air, but does this have anything to do with outsourcing and end-user and supplier partnerships? The instinctive reaction is yes, it does, but it is difficult sometimes to be specific and produce hard evidence to support this feeling.

Babin and Nicholson have undertaken a unique program of field-based research to try and do just that. By applying rigorous academic techniques in a real-world business context, they studied in depth an organization with a long history of ethical business-based practices – the financial services arm of the Co-operative Group, which was founded in 1844 and is widely regarded as the first successful co-operative movement. It is right to say that compassionate capitalism is not a new concept to the co-op, even if the term is. Being an ethical organization does not mean that there is any inbuilt bias against outsourcing or offshoring, far from it in fact. Part of being sustainable is being financially and operationally sustainable too, and outsourcing can actively support these requirements, but it must be done in a way which is complementary to the ethical agenda. Of course if you are outsourcing then you have by definition a relationship with a third party, and Babin and Nicholson studied in the same way one of the key long-term partners used by the co-op, Steria.

By looking in depth at both parties beyond the contract and at commercial constructs of the relationship, Babin and Nicholson looked for evidence of a broader benefits construct that would apply to both parties, but with an ethical focus, and tried to determine whether benefits could be observed and determined in a way which would ultimately enable organizations to strategically plan such engagements, as opposed to retrospective observation, thus moving into proactive strategic differentiation and leverage. As the sponsor for this work within the Co-operative I am pleased to say that I think that the authors have been able to do just that. They have applied sound modeling techniques to a real-world business situation and determined that it is indeed possible to work ethically and strategically within the globalized outsourcing model in such a way that both organizations can benefit beyond the traditional supplier–buyer axis. In today's world of compassionate capitalism this is indeed a significant step forward. Therefore this book is for you if you want an evidence-based approach to strategically planning mutual benefits from collaborative ethical initiatives in the globalized outsourcing arena.

It was personally a great pleasure to work with both the authors and I am pleased that we have between us moved an important agenda forward. I hope that you too feel the same after reading this book.

Steve Briggs
Head of IT Strategic Partnerships
Co-operative Banking Group
January 2012

Glossary of Terms

Term	Abbreviation	Description	Key authors
Business Process Outsourcing	BPO	The outsourcing of business services that have previously been performed within an organization. Usually the business services are standardized across many organizations so that a common service can be delivered by one outsourcing provider to many buyers. For example, payroll and accounting business processes are frequently outsourced.	Kotlarsky Oshri
Carbon Disclosure Project	CDP	An organization that collects and reports greenhouse gas emission data from more than 2,500 organizations "in order that they can set reduction targets and make performance improvements".	
Carbon Reduction Commitment	CRC	An initiative of the UK government to reduce greenhouse gas emissions by at least 80% by 2050. The Climate Change Bill became law on 26 November 2008. CRC will result in mandatory public reporting of energy efficiency, plus incentives and penalties.	
Corporate Social and Environmental Responsibility	CSER	An outsourcing buyer and an outsourcing provider working together in a project with common goals to improve an agreed topic that has a positive impact on society and/or on the environment.	Babin Nicholson

Corporate Social Responsibility	CSR	The responsibility of organizations to provide more than economic returns to shareholders, to be responsible for contributions to stakeholders in society, including citizens, governments, unions, NGOs and others.	Carroll Matten Moon
Global IT Outsourcing	GITO	Third-party management of IT assets and services, including people and knowledge content, which are delivered in a coordinated fashion across multiple international locations.	Carmel Hirschheim Kotlarsky Lacity Nicholson Oshri Rottman Willcocks
Global Reporting Initiative	GRI	A reporting standard for social and environmental responsibility. Established in 1997 "to address sustainability challenges such as global climate change", GRI provides a "trusted and credible framework for sustainability reporting that can be used by organizations of any size, sector or location". GRI is now broadly recognized by many organizations as a standard for corporate responsibility and sustainability reporting.	
Green IT		A term broadly used to identify information technology (IT) products and services that are increasingly efficient in consumption of natural resources and with reduced impact on the environment. The term is also used to describe the use of IT to reduce carbon emissions in business operations.	
ISO 26000 Guidance for Social Responsibility		An overall standard for social responsibility, including subjects on governance, human rights, labor practices, the environment, fair operating practices, consumer issues, community involvement and development.	

(Continued)

Term	Abbreviation	Description	Key authors
Outsourcing arrangement		A contract between an outsourcing buyer and provider to deliver services at an agreed price over a defined period of time.	
Responsive CSR		CSR projects that focus on compliance, or on acting as a good corporate citizen, responding to the evolving social and environmental concerns of stakeholders.	Kramer Porter
Stages of Growth	SOG	A theoretical model that describes the stages or periods of time, in the development of a concept, such as sustainability or trust. A set of characteristics identify the start and end of each stage, with rapid growth in between, typically referred to as an 'S' curve. The model is useful in identifying when one stage has finished and the next is about to begin.	Nolan
Strategic CSR		CSR projects are initiatives where the social, environmental and business benefits are large, distinctive over a long period of time and aligned with the corporate strategy.	Kramer Porter
SA 8000		Social Accountability International (SAI) labor standards for the global manufacturing industry. SA 8000 assures consumers that products and services are delivered from facilities with fair working conditions for employees.	
Sustainability		Development that meets the needs of the present without compromising the ability of future generations to meet their own needs, as defined by the UN Brundtland report. Sustainability implies a voluntary contribution for social and environmental well-being by an organization to a broad set of stakeholders.	Brundtland Elkington Emerson

Triple Bottom Line	TBL	A concept where organizations measure their economic (profit), social (people) and environmental (planet) performance. TPL is often referred to as the three 'P's: profit, people and planet.	Elkington
Trust		A characteristic of the working relationship between two organizations, that is an outsourcing buyer and an outsourcing provider, that helps to maintain strong and effective collaboration between the two parties.	Bunker Lewicki Rousseau

Introduction: Achieving Social and Environmental Responsibility in Global Outsourcing

Why is sustainability, also known as corporate social and environmental responsibility (CSER), important in global information technology (IT) outsourcing? Our extensive research over five years, including hundreds of interviews with outsourcing buyers, providers and advisers, provides answers to that question. Most importantly, this research describes the competitive benefits that accrue to outsourcing providers and buyers when they collaborate on sustainability issues. After reading this book, you will understand how collaborative sustainability can create benefits not only for your outsourcing relationship, wider society and the environment.

Global IT outsourcing (GITO), refers to third-party management of IT assets and services, including hardware, software, people and knowledge content, which are delivered in a coordinated fashion across multiple international locations. IT assets include hardware such as computer data centers, desktop and personal computers, communications devices and networks. IT assets also include software such as in-house application software and commercially purchased software. IT services include software development and maintenance as well as testing, documentation management, research and operation of IT hardware and infrastructure assets. Outsourcing of IT and business processes has just over a 20-year history, beginning in the early 1990s. Sustainability is the recognition that all organizations have an obligation to use the resources of society and the planet responsibly, so that future generations will continue to prosper. In the late 1980s, the United Nations (UN) coined the term "sustainability" to address global environment and development concerns. The concept of sustainability is broad, as we will discuss below, with many interpretations and points of view. Recognition of the importance of sustainability has grown in tandem with the growth of outsourcing as organizations realize

1

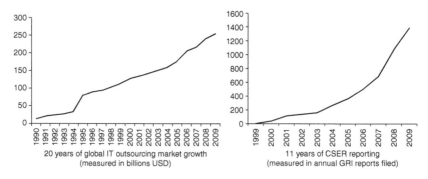

Figure I.1   The rise of GITO and sustainability reporting
Source: Willcocks and Lacity (2010); Global Reporting Initiative (2009).

that they must use natural resources, including people and societies, in a way that will not diminish the ability to sustain future development.

Figure I.1 depicts the parallel rise of global outsourcing and sustainability reporting. In 1990, the global outsourcing market had just begun; in 1999, the first Global Reporting Initiative (GRI) sustainability report was registered. Since these two dates, both phenomena have grown at tremendous rates with similar growth curves.

Despite solid and growing bodies of research on outsourcing and on sustainability, there has been limited research on the intersection of these two concepts. This book explores their intersection and addresses a key management issue as sustainability becomes increasingly important to buyers and providers of outsourcing services as well as their many stakeholders, including employees, governments, shareholders and society in general.

The objective of this book is to provide an understanding, drawn from current buyers and providers of outsourcing services, of how sustainability considerations are factored into the outsourcing relationship. This includes both new arrangements and the renewal of existing outsourcing arrangements. In short, what is the importance of sustainability in outsourcing? Four further questions extend from this:

1) What, if any, are the benefits of sustainability in an outsourcing relationship, for buyers and providers?
2) How should outsourcing providers develop sustainability within their organizations?
3) How should outsourcing buyers evaluate providers from a sustainability perspective?

4) What is the role of emerging global sustainability standards (such as the GRI and the ISO 26000 Guidance for Social Responsibility) and government regulations and guidelines?

Integration of Outsourcing and Sustainability

Buyers and providers of outsourcing services have increasingly embraced sustainability issues. Since our early reports on this topic starting in 2008 the volume and intensity of sustainability discussion in GITO has grown considerably. For example,

- the International Association of Outsourcing Professionals (IAOP) established a Corporate Social Responsibility Committee in 2009, with the goal of defining a guide for the outsourcing industry;
- the Global Sourcing Council (GSC) recognizes leaders in sustainability with an annual Sustainable and Socially Responsible Sourcing (3S) award;
- in 2010, the IAOP began to evaluate the sustainability profile of applicants to the Global Outsourcing Top 100; and
- India's software and service companies trade association, NASSCOM, has established a green IT initiative and has established the NASSCOM Foundation "with the aim to use information and communication technologies for development and to catalyze the CSR arena within the Indian IT industry".[1]

These examples demonstrate the growing interest in sustainability to the outsourcing industry. We have seen a steady growth in sustainability announcements from major outsourcing providers such as Accenture, IBM and a large Indian GITO provider, as these providers recognize that outsourcing buyers expect and favor a stronger sustainability profile in their providers. Consulting firms such as Accenture have recognized that outsourcing buyers are also in need of consulting advice and implementation assistance in this new area.

As further evidence of the growth of sustainability in GITO, a 2009 IAOP[2] survey on social responsibility in outsourcing found that CSR "is an important and growing issue for outsourcing customers and providers – 71% say that CSR will become more important or much more important in future outsourcing contracts".[3] When outsourcing buyers and providers rated the importance of sustainability in their business strategy, the response was 3.9 on a 5-point scale, where 1 was somewhat important and 5 was crucial.

Respondents to the IAOP survey rated social issues as more important than environmental issues. The top three sustainability issues that outsourcing buyers look for are labor practices, fair operating practices and respect for human rights. Comparing the 2009 IAOP survey of CSR in Outsourcing to the 2011 survey, the number of buyers who evaluate CSR capabilities in outsourcing providers jumped from 8% to 23% of respondents, whereas those who never consider CSR capabilities reduced from 12% to 3%.[4] Clearly, the uptake of CSR and sustainability is a growing topic in the outsourcing market.

GITO is a well-established business practice that offers reduced costs and improved performance, stimulates creativity, gives access to new capacity in resources and improves shareholder value. In the early years of GITO, during the 1990s and early 2000s, managers and executives were often challenged to demonstrate the rationale and strategy for outsourcing IT and IT-enabled services such as finance, accounting and human resource processes. Today, outsourcing is generally accepted as a management tactic to improve organizational performance. In many industries, outsourcing has become the norm for processes that are not part of an organization's core competency.

The Outsourcing Unit at the London School of Economics, UK, has found outsourcing to be part of forward-looking strategy for many companies. Its research shows that across all sectors, properly planned, adequately resourced and managed outsourcing can deliver significant competitive advantage to companies and organizations.[5]

A significant academic and practitioner literature has emerged over the last 20 years, which has improved our understanding of the management of GITO relationships.[6] Global outsourcing continues to grow. The majority of the companies included on the Fortune 500 list are already buyers of GITO and/or business process outsourcing (BPO) and the market is expanding. In 2008, the GITO market was valued at between $220 and $250 billion.[7] The estimate for 2009–2014 is that GITO will grow by 6–9% per annum, whereas mainstream BPO expenditure is likely to grow worldwide by 10–15% a year, from $140 billion in 2005 to more than $230 billion by 2013.[8] In India, NASSCOM reported that worldwide BPO spending grew by 12% in 2008, and that the IT and business services market is expected to grow almost fivefold by 2018.[9] The IAOP's "Outsourcing 2010 State of the Industry Survey", authored by Accenture, found that organizations had increased their intentions to expand their existing outsourcing programs from 38% in January 2009 to 56% in January 2010. The IAOP survey additionally reported that "by a 2-to-1 margin, customers say they've been increasing the volume of work and scope of services being outsourced.[10] Most organizations now accept that some aspect of their business, either small or large, can be outsourced".

What is sustainability?

The term sustainability is frequently used but poorly defined. The two key elements of sustainability are society and the environment, that is corporate sustainability reflects a company's acknowledged responsibility to people and to the planet. Sustainability was initially defined in the 1980s in the UN Report of the World Commission on Environment and Development[11] and broadly included development of topics such as the environment, population and human resources, species and ecosystems, energy and food security. The report of the Brundtland Commission "Our Common Future", published in 1987, defined sustainability as "development that meets the needs of the present without compromising the ability of future generations to meet their own needs".

The idea of sustainability evolved in the 1990s to include the concepts of CSR and the triple bottom line.[12] CSR is a broad management topic with many different interpretations. Researchers Archie Carroll[13] and John Elkington describe CSR as the responsibility of organizations to provide more than economic returns to shareholders. John Elkington coined the term "triple bottom line", referring to the need for organizations to focus equally on profits, people and the planet.[14] Thus, sustainability can be understood as a broad concept that includes social (people) and environmental (planet) issues.

In the past, the terms were separate: sustainability related to the environment only and CSR referred to social aspects, such as human rights. Today, sustainability is often depicted as a combination of both CSR and environmental responsibility. However, although literature on sustainability and CSR both tend to address aspects of the human population, sustainability papers focus to a greater extent on the measurable aspects of the human population, such as population density, access to clean water, availability of food and availability of clean air. CSR literature tends to be published in management journals and focuses on the balance between business and society, and the impact of business practices on society, including individuals, families and communities. Many organizations have adopted different names to convey their social and environmental responsibilities. A review of the GRI listing for 2010 identified 368 reports whose title, in English, includes the words "corporate responsibility", or CSR, or "social responsibility" and "social report". From the same 2010 GRI list, 543 reports contained the word "sustainability" or "sustainable" in the report title.[15] The ratio of CSR reports to sustainability reports is 40:60, suggesting that "sustainability" is the more popular term. Figure I.2 shows the overlap of social and environmental responsibility.

Here, we use the term sustainability to mean social and environmental responsibility and identify specifics of either CSR or environmental considerations where applicable. The social issues related to outsourcing include employment, fair wages and working conditions, education, worker health and safety and community involvement. Environmental issues include power consumption and related greenhouse gas (GHG) emissions, as well as the environmental footprint of the outsourcing provider such as air travel, water consumption and electronic waste.

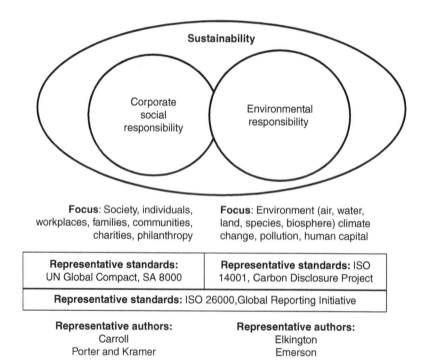

Figure I.2   Overlap of CSR, environmental responsibility and sustainability
Source: Carroll (1991); Porter and Kramer (2006); Elkington (1994); Emerson (2003).

Why should we care about sustainability and outsourcing?

The intersection of sustainability and outsourcing is important for four reasons. First, with pressure from stakeholder groups such as customers and labor unions, outsourcing buyers increasingly expect that providers are able to live up to sustainability expectations. Second, governments and regulators are defining sustainability requirements, especially in the area of the environmental responsibility, which will require compliance from outsourcing providers. Third, non-governmental organizations (NGOs) such as the United Nations, Greenpeace and Ceres have established sustainability standards that are increasingly used to measure the performance of large, global organizations such as outsourcing providers (see Chapters 1 and 2). Fourth, proactive outsourcing buyers and providers are adopting sustainability abilities that give them a competitive benefit in the outsourcing market (see Chapters 3–5).

Businesses are increasingly embracing sustainability. In 2010, the World Business Council for Sustainable Development (WBCSD) published "Vision 2050".[16] The WBCSD report suggests that in 40 years the world's population will have increased by 30% to 9 billion, challenging our ability to attain or maintain "the consumptive lifestyle" that we know today. The WBCSD stresses the need for businesses to address the interconnected issues of water, food and energy in a holistic way. Notably, two global outsourcing providers, Accenture and a large Indian GITO provider, contributed to the sustainability goals of Vision 2050, along with 27 other global organizations. Also notable is WBCSD's inclusion of social issues such as education and health, in addition to environmental issues, under the definition of sustainability.

Looking at global outsourcing from the perspective of sustainability reveals how outsourcing affects a broader set of stakeholders than just shareholders. The costs of outsourcing to both local and global society and to the environment are weighed against the benefits to the organizations and their shareholders. A rising wave of sustainability concerns has encouraged organizations to examine the social and environmental implications of their outsourcing business decisions.

Social responsibility issues related to outsourcing provoke strong reactions from the public and governments. The range of opinion is wide and, although there are "shades of grey", they can broadly be identified as pessimistic and optimistic. Pessimists fear that outsourcing encourages unfettered capitalism and irresponsible corporate profit maximization that increases the income inequalities between the developed and developing worlds. Optimists argue that outsourcing is beneficial because it distributes work and income globally.

Outsourcing pessimists argue that outsourcing maximizes profit for the rich and offers limited or no benefits for other groups. As evidence, they point to the growing gap between rich and poor in developing countries, saying the rich simply get richer as a result of outsourcing, exacerbating income inequality in both the developing and the developed world in an increasingly information-based economy.[17] They believe that ongoing and increasing levels of global outsourcing will have disruptive effects.[18] North America and Europe will, they claim, experience significant displacement of a broad range of workers, many from upper educational reaches, who will be neither passive nor politically quiet. Pessimists wonder whether the seeds of a future social and political crisis are being sown as millions of white-collar workers face unemployment.[19] Others suggest that although outsourcing allows companies to reduce their wage burdens, which may benefit shareholders, the host country or employer may not experience concurrent benefits, and those workers displaced by the outsourcing may not easily be able to transition to highly skilled jobs.[20] Some argue that transnational corporations create global labor pools, where they take advantage of those with fewer employment opportunities, provide little regulatory protection and have weak social safety nets, which reduce the bargaining power of all employees.

Global outsourcing optimists view outsourcing as a mechanism for sharing wealth on a global basis. They propose that sustainability and ethical trading, especially for global consumer-branded products and services, as well as collective action toward the International Labour Organization's fair-work agenda, can improve labor conditions.[21] Optimists perceive global outsourcing as beneficial and

> clearly ethically justified... outsourcing promotes efficiency; helps developing countries by providing jobs where unemployment is very high, involves transfer of information technology and knowledge and encourages the educational process in less developed countries so that people are trained for new types of work provided by information technology and helps cut the costs of goods and services.[22]

Several authors provide a more balanced assessment, suggesting that outsourcing is inevitable but can be conducted fairly and perhaps with benefits to many global stakeholders. Researchers at the University of Hertfordshire in the United Kingdom suggest that organizations should expect to manage outsourcing risk issues by embracing sustainability. Although outsourcing is a fundamental business strategy that has existed for 20 years, the pace and nature of outsourcing has dramatically increased through the use of low-cost electronic communications and global computing abilities.[23] Outsourcing, when used properly, can provide long-term operational and business improvements.

Outsourcing also creates risks. Human resources are fundamentally important to the success of any organization, and by externalizing these resources through outsourcing, an organization takes on a higher risk, with an expectation of improved capability. A key ethical consideration for outsourcing and offshoring is worker exploitation, because the expectation of low prices often requires low wages and poor working conditions, and engenders fierce competition among providers from national and developing countries.[24] Researchers at the University of Hertfordshire conclude with a suggestion that ethical outsourcing requires an agreement between corporations, their shareholders, employees, governments and civil society, that all parties will benefit from the outsourcing agreement.

In summary, both pessimistic and optimistic opinion leaders and researchers are paying considerable attention to the topic of social responsibility in outsourcing. Sustainability presents challenges to outsourcing providers and buyers, both of which must have the business knowledge and abilities to understand and address the social issues related to outsourcing. Government and non-governmental organizations have begun to define and monitor standards for corporate social activities, which are applicable in varying degrees to outsourcing providers. Outsourcing providers and buyers must also have the knowledge and capability to understand and ensure compliance with appropriate sustainability standards.

1
Why Is Sustainable Outsourcing Important?

> Sustainable outsourcing opens up life opportunities for people in India who would otherwise have much less.
>
> M. Ellison, Senior Manager, Co-operative Financial Services

> Sustainability is embedded in the measurement of every individual, that's what they, and our vendors, have to do to be successful in our world.
>
> Jim Slack, CIO, Co-operative Financial Services

> Sustainability issues do not go away [with outsourcing]. They are complex and inter-related, across all business sectors.
>
> Sustainability Lead, IBM Canada

Outsourcing success is never guaranteed. The Outsourcing Center and the Farmer School of Business Administration at Miami University, Florida, USA,[1] examined the causes of outsourcing failure and found that 11% of the 256 respondents identified poor communication as a frequent cause of outsourcing failure, whereas 40% of the respondents believed that better communication would add more value to the outsourcing relationship. According to the Outsourcing Unit at the London School of Economics, UK, "The outsourcing highway is littered with casualties." It cites multiple examples of outsourcing failure since 2000,[2] including the following:

- UK retailer Sainsbury's, which announced in 2004–2005 a write-off of $254 million of IT assets and a further $218 million write-off of automated depot and supply-chain IT, the aftermath of a failed seven-year deal to outsource its IT operations;

- US financial services firm JPMorgan Chase & Co., which scrapped a $5 billion contract in 2004 with the intention of moving the IT work back in-house; and
- the remarks made by the chairman of a powerful UK House of Commons committee, who described an American outsourcing company as "cowboys who should be run out of town" over their handling of the Lorenzo electronic patient record system for that country's National Health Service.[3]

There is no "magic bullet" to avoid these types of failures, but there is considerable evidence that activities that reduce risk and improve the buyer–provider outsourcing relationship will be welcomed.[4] We have found that sustainability projects that are shared between buyers and providers, which we call collaborative sustainability, will improve communication and trust between the two parties. Improved trust improves the likelihood of success in an outsourcing arrangement.

Sustainability in GITO is also important because of the growing expectations of stakeholders, including buyers, governments, employees and shareholders. As many organizations and their stakeholders increase their expectations regarding social and environmental issues, buyer sustainability expectations will inevitably be applied to outsourcing providers. For example, Walmart's Green Goods environmental campaign[5] has had a significant impact on its supply partners. Similarly, IT or business process outsourcing providers, whether operating onshore, nearshore or offshore (e.g. in India),[6] should expect to be held to the same level of sustainability performance to which their customers aspire.

GITO providers must increasingly consider issues of sustainability in their service offerings. Buyers, governments, employees and even NGOs are expecting GITO providers to behave in ways that are socially and environmentally responsible. Buyers want a provider who can bring sustainability improvements and leading global best practices to the relationship. Governments require measurable improvements in carbon efficiency, often driven by IT services. Employees want to work in organizations that demonstrate leadership in social and environmental issues. NGOs such as Greenpeace expect outsourcing providers to develop solutions to global sustainability problems and to demonstrate sustainability leadership in their operations. For example, Greenpeace monitors sustainability performance with its Cool IT Challenge, which challenges IT companies to combat climate change through technological advancements that benefit both the company and the environment.[7] Outsourcing providers are already reacting to stakeholder sustainability expectations and many comply with government sustainability regulations (see Chapter 3).

Let us take a look at the evolution of sustainability into a management buzzword and investigate the reason it has gained momentum in outsourcing.

Corporate social responsibility

Early discussions on CSR were a precursor to today's sustainability debate. In the 40 years since the economist Milton Friedman[8] argued that the sole purpose of business is to increase profits for its owners, excluding any involvement with, or contribution to, social or community causes, the role and concept of CSR has evolved considerably.[9] In 1991 Archie Carroll set out a basic set of ideas called the Pyramid of CSR, which shows a hierarchy from legal and ethical requirements to voluntary philanthropy[10] (see Figure 1.1).

Since Carroll's publication, many scholars have attempted to better understand the significance of CSR to an organization. Mintzberg, Rendtorff and other management researchers[11] point to the increasing need for organizations and their leaders to challenge self-interest and to balance the syndrome of organizational selfishness with social responsibility and cooperative human engagement. Others have posited that organizations can "do well by doing good" and that "practicing CSR is not altruistic do-gooding, but rather a way for both companies and society to prosper".[12] In particular, the work of Jed Emerson has highlighted the importance of blending both social and economic returns from investments.[13] He describes the importance of CSR as more than a voluntary philanthropic

Pyramid level	Responsibility	Description
Pinnacle	Philanthropy	Give time and money to worthy charities in the community
Level 3	Ethical	Perform beyond the requirements of the law, doing what society judges to be right, just and fair
Level 2	Legal	Obey the law
Foundation	Economic	Provide ongoing economic return to shareholders and other stakeholders, such as employees, suppliers, lenders, etc.

Figure 1.1 The Pyramid of CSR
Source: Adapted from *Carroll, Business Horizons, 34, 1991.*

activity, with management weighing the social and environmental impact of their firm's activities as part of the overall strategy for unlocking value.

Recent discussion has focused on how CSR can lead to the strengthening of a firm's long-term competitiveness.[14] The strategic use of CSR, where it can be used for long-term competitive advantage to distinguish one organization from its competitors, has become an important theme in the "do well by doing good" management literature. The use of CSR for competitive advantage differs from the voluntary philanthropic approach described by Carroll. Michael Porter and Mark Kramer from Harvard Business School, USA, have built linkages between their work on firm competitiveness and CSR. These authors describe the concept of creating value through "focused philanthropy" to create a new set of strategic management tools that strengthen an organization's competitiveness. In their recent papers, they have focused on a CSR program's contribution to new opportunity, innovation and competitive advantage to a firm. They argue that prevailing justifications for CSR, such as moral obligation and reputation, have created "muddled" corporate responsibility thinking. Instead, the authors advocate evaluating CSR opportunities that create shared value, positively affecting both business and society. They propose a responsive strategic CSR framework (see Figure 1.2). Essentially, they argue that organizations should adopt strategic CSR initiatives that "unlock shared value by investing in social aspects of context that strengthen company competitiveness". They suggest that creating shared value between business and society will create an expanded pool of economic and social value to combat the

The CSR framework

Good citizenship

Strategic philanthropy

Responsive   Strategic

Figure 1.2   Responsive / strategic CSR model
Source: Authors, adapted from Porter and Kramer (2006).

weakened connection between firms and their community brought about by a greater reliance on outside vendors, outsourcing and offshoring.

Socially responsible outsourcing

How has CSR entered into outsourcing? One route is via socially responsible outsourcing (SRO), which is an outsourcing model that is, according to Samasource CEO Leila Chirayath Janah, "a social business helping bright but marginalized people in poor regions find dignified jobs by expanding their access to markets".[15] Samasource, a non-profit organization that connects people living in poverty to computer-based work via the Internet, defines its mission as: "to reduce poverty by connecting marginalized people to training and remote work opportunities online". Typically, an SRO firm will be located in a marginalized region and will employ people from a disadvantaged population, for example uneducated women in India or Africa. In these arrangements, a third party may intervene to manage the relationship. The Rockefeller Foundation impact sourcing model, described below, is an example of a third-party intervention to encourage SRO. Case study 6.3 in Chapter 6 describes how a social enterprise has intervened to create outsourcing businesses for women in Kerala, India. SRO is a specific application of sustainability in outsourcing. The concept of SRO is closely related to the use of information and communications technologies (ICT) for developing nations, sometimes referred to as ICT4D.[16] Another implementation of SRO, called rural sourcing, locates outsourced services in remote areas of a particular country.[17] The rural-source model has the benefit of keeping outsourcing workers within the national boundaries of the buyer, while still achieving lower costs through outsourcing. SRO is attracting the interest of high-profile and influential NGOs. The Rockefeller Foundation, working with the Monitor consulting company, has identified the concept of Impact Sourcing, a form of SRO, "to create sustainable jobs that can generate step-function income improvement for those at the base of the pyramid, defined as individuals who live on annual incomes of less than $3,000 of local purchasing power".[18] With the emphasis and support of the Rockefeller Foundation we expect to see a growing awareness and interest in SRO.

What is sustainable global outsourcing?

As members of the global value chain, buyers expect outsourcing providers to be held to the same level of social and environmental responsibility, that is sustainability, that their customers expect of them. Therefore, many buyers have increased their sustainability expectations for providers. For example, in July 2009, Walmart introduced an environmental responsibility index to assess its 100,000 suppliers around the world, requiring them to report their environmental responsibility plans, including carbon disclosure. Walmart is the largest private user of electricity in the United States and is intent on reducing its own environmental footprint as well as that of its suppliers. Walmart is doing this both to lower its costs, by, for example, reducing packaging and fuel consumption, and to respond to its customers who frequently ask for sustainability improvements. This is consistent with advice gathered from our own research and that of others[19] who argue that organizations should develop sustainable operations by analyzing each link in the value chain.

Four global IT outsourcing environmental sustainability issues

The four environmental sustainability issues that are of key concern to buyers and providers of GITO include power consumption, travel requirements, water supply and electronic waste.

1) **Power.** The power consumption of ICT continues to increase with the proliferation of ICT in business. Large IT outsourcing providers consume significant electrical power to operate the ICT infrastructure. Electrical power usually requires the burning of carbon fuels, which in turn produce GHGs. In addition, the cost of electricity continues to rise as the number of servers and related equipment used increases. As a result, many IT outsourcing providers are taking steps to source greener electricity and to reduce consumption.
2) **Travel.** The volume of employee travel required for the management of global outsourcing[20] is an environmental concern due to the production of GHGs by aircraft and other means of transportation.
3) **Water.** The availability and conservation of fresh water for the large number of employees and communities in outsourcing provider delivery centers is a sustainability concern in India, a major GITO location.
4) **Electronic waste.** The "e-waste" from end-of-life ICT such as servers, PCs and communication devices is a significant sustainability issue.

Below, we expand on each of these issues.

Energy consumption and GHG emissions

Most outsourcing providers are major consumers of electrical power. The increasing power consumption by information technology infrastructure, which doubled from 2000 to 2005, according to the US Environmental Protection Agency, gives rise to two environmental concerns related to IT outsourcing:

1) **The cost of energy impacts IT operations.** The 2009 Green Outsourcing Survey reported that 85% of the senior executives surveyed said that "the adoption of green technology is more likely the result of escalating energy costs than ecological altruism"; and
2) **Most electricity generation produces GHGs.** GHGs have been linked to global warming. It has been estimated that 85% of global energy consumption "is represented by fossil energy, with oil, gas, and coal contributing roughly equal amounts" and "our energy problem lies in the effects caused by CO_2 produced when fossil fuels are burned".[21]

Data centers have an unrelenting appetite for energy. According to an influential study, total power used by information technology equipment in data centers during 2005 represented about 0.5% of the world's electricity consumption.[22] When cooling and auxiliary infrastructure are included, that figure is about 1%. Data from the same study states that aggregate electricity for servers doubled over the period 2000–2005 both in the United States and worldwide, and that almost all of this growth was the result of growth in the number of servers. In the period 2005–2010, electricity used by data centers worldwide increased by about 56%, whereas in the United States it increased by about 36%. The estimate provided for electricity use by data centers in 2010 represents about 1.3% of all electricity use for the world and 2% of all electricity use for the United States.[23] And these estimates exclude electricity use for ICT outside of data centers, such as for desktop and laptop computers, local printers, servers and communication devices. Another study estimates that all computer-related equipment and Internet usage is responsible for close to 6% of US electricity consumption.[24] These figures present a wide variation in the share of ICT in total electrical power consumption, from a low of 1% to a high of 6%. There are two key implications of this:

• ICT proliferation over the last two decades has been significant and continues to grow, with an "eightfold" increase in the number of PCs and a "325-fold increase" in Internet usage.[25] The aggregate consumption of electricity by ICT devices inside and outside of data centers will continue to grow; and

- the implication for outsourcing providers is that governments and regulators will increasingly examine and regulate electrical power consumption for ICT services. The European Union has defined data center energy standards, and the UK government has established a Carbon Reduction Commitment (CRC) to reduce overall electrical power consumption, as the following case illustrates.

Case 1.1: The European Commission and the UK Government Regulate Data Center Power Consumption

The European Commission's Institute for Energy's "Code of Conduct on Data Centres Energy Efficiency"[26] attempts to address the problem of growing data center energy consumption. The code states that

> The projected energy consumption rise poses a problem for European Union energy and environmental policies. It is important that the energy efficiency of data centers is maximized to ensure the carbon emissions and other impacts such as strain on infrastructure associated with increases in energy consumption are mitigated.

This voluntary code defines best practices and commitments for industry and governments. Several European countries have established policies for carbon emission reductions that have an impact on data centers. For example, the UK government created the CRC to reduce GHG emissions by at least 80% by 2050. According to the Department of Energy and Climate Change, "The UK has passed legislation which introduces the world's first long-term legally binding framework to tackle the dangers of climate change. The Climate Change Bill became law on 26 November 2008." CRC will be mandatory for UK data centers that consume more than 6,000 MWh and will result in mandatory public reporting of energy efficiency, plus incentives and penalties.

As governments enact legislation to mandate improved energy efficiency, most if not all organizations will be challenged to reduce their overall ICT carbon footprint. Data centers and other electricity-intensive ICT facilities will become obvious targets for sustainability standards and legislation.

Global outsourcing does not solve the energy consumption problem, as it simply moves the problem from an in-house data center to an outsourced facility, often in a distant global location. In the United Kingdom, outsourcing providers face penalties under the CRC legislation when contracted to undertake responsibility for a client's data center because that will increase its carbon emissions. Similarly, a buyer who outsources a data center to an offshore location will be acknowledged as having reduced carbon emissions in the United Kingdom, even though the offshore GITO provider may have a worse carbon emission record. The UK National Outsourcing Association (NOA) has called for a single international uniform standard of measurement for carbon efficiency in global outsourcing, "a definitive green standard that all organizations can engage with ... to be internationally regulated and approved so that there can be a level playing field within the global market".[27] This statement from a professional association underlines the importance of anticipating regulation of energy consumption and GHG emissions for the outsourcing industry.

Travel and water consumption – The impact of humans on the environment

Global IT outsourcing providers have two additional environmental impacts that can be measured: the amount of travel (and related GHG emissions) undertaken by and the amount of fresh water consumption by employees. Air travel is a significant aspect of global outsourcing, especially when developing new business relationships. Researchers at Cranfield University, UK,[28] found that 57% of business people travel for new business relationships (e.g. to sell to a new IT outsourcing buyer), whereas day-to-day management and operations require far less travel. Given the global nature of outsourcing, flying is the predominant mode of travel in the outsourcing business. The Cranfield researchers state that air travel contributes significantly to an organization's carbon footprint, and for service firms such as consultancies, "travel may account for as much as half of the company's carbon emissions". As will be described in Chapter 3, a large Indian GITO provider tracks individual employee carbon emissions, particularly air travel. This is one example of a GITO provider that is taking steps to reduce its own carbon emissions and in doing so improve its sustainability profile.

In many parts of the world, per capita availability of fresh water will decrease as the human population grows.[29] For global IT outsourcers in areas of the world such as India, where fresh water is not plentiful, conservation of water is an important sustainability issue. In many cases, outsourcing providers have hired thousands of personnel at global delivery centers, creating significant water requirements. A large Indian outsourcing and training center that we visited near Bangalore, India, was built on a greenfield site and resembled University. Ten thousand employees are housed on the campus that includes office space, recreational facilities and food service areas. The Indian outsourcing provider has committed to a "water-neutral" environment, so that all fresh water is captured in dedicated reservoirs and a significant proportion is recycled.

e-Waste

A final GITO-related environmental concern is e-waste. Several jurisdictions have recognized the growing problem of e-waste and have enacted legislation that requires a planned and environmentally appropriate method for disposal of obsolete electronic equipment. In the United States, 19 states have passed legislation mandating e-waste recycling programs. In Canada, the Ontario government has enacted the Waste Diversion Act, which resulted in the industry-led Waste Electrical and Electronic Equipment Program (WEEE). This program requires buyers of electronic equipment to pay an upfront disposal fee for equipment such as computers, printers, monitors, etc. The state of California has a consumer electronic waste recycling fee similar to that of the Canadian program. The European Union has also developed policy and legislation – as the following case shows.

Case 1.2: European Parliament legislates for e-waste

In January 2003, the European Parliament enacted the WEEE Directive, which prohibits end-users from disposing of electrical and electronic equipment as household waste. To achieve this objective, producers of electrical and electronic equipment became responsible for treatment, recovery and financing aspects related to the recycling of their products. By 2009, all 27 European Union member states had implemented a national WEEE legislation.

Global sustainability standards

The challenges posed by GITO-related sustainability issues are beginning to be addressed by "an increasing number of social responsibility standards, watchdogs, auditors and certifiers aiming at institutionalizing and harmonizing practices globally".[30] Several industries, such as the mining industry and apparel manufacturing industry, have created industry-specific sustainability standards and codes of conduct. Many of these standards were developed in response to pressure from unions, NGOs and multi-stakeholder organizations. Some authors[31] have predicted an increase in the quantity and quality of environmental reporting in response to demands from customer and investor stakeholders. To date, the outsourcing industry has not defined sustainability standards, but the following four global standards are relevant candidates.

1) **Global Reporting Initiative (GRI)** was established in 1997 as an initiative of Ceres, a not-for-profit organization formed to work with other organizations to focus on sustainability issues, including global climate change. In 1999, GRI collected sustainability reports from nine organizations; 11 years later, the 2010 GRI index collects sustainability reports from more than 1,800 organizations. GRI gathers information from organizations on their environmental, social and governance performance, which "can be used to demonstrate organizational commitment to sustainable development, to compare organizational performance over time, and to measure organizational performance with respect to laws, norms, standards and voluntary initiatives".[32] GRI is now broadly recognized by many organizations as a standard for corporate responsibility and sustainability reporting, and it serves as a public record of organizations that have voluntarily provided their sustainability reports.
2) **Carbon Disclosure Project (CDP)** is an NGO that collects and reports GHG emission data from more than 2,500 organizations to help them establish and achieve target carbon emission reductions. The number of CDP-participating organizations increased from 235 in 2003 to 2,456 in 2009, a tenfold increase in six years.
    The following two global sustainability standards do not have annual reporting requirements like GRI and CDP. Instead, participating organizations are compliance-certified.
3) **United Nations Global Compact** is "a strategic policy initiative, for businesses that are committed to aligning their operations and strategies with ten universally accepted principles in the areas of human rights,

labour, environment and anti-corruption"[33]. It is focused on businesses and requires CEO endorsement. The Compact's overarching mission is to help build a more sustainable and inclusive global economy. In 2010, GRI and the UN Global Compact announced an agreement,[34] whereby the 5,800 business signatories to the UN Global Compact agreed to use the GRI sustainability guidelines, increasing the number of GRI annual reports.

4) **International Standards Organization (ISO) ISO 26000** is an overall standard for social responsibility. This standard provides a guide for organizations which voluntarily adopt sustainability practices. ISO 26000 addresses core sustainability subjects, including governance, human rights, labour practices, the environment, fair operating practices, consumer issues, community involvement and development. With participation from about 80 countries and many stakeholder groups, it is expected that ISO 26000 will be recognized as a universal standard across most industries. ISO 26000 was ratified as a voluntary standard in 2010, having been in development since 2005.

Seven reasons to embrace sustainability in outsourcing

This section describes our research, which began in 2008, with interviews with North American, European and UK-based outsourcing buyers, providers and advisors, from which we could distill seven main reasons why sustainability is a high priority for chief executive officers (Table 1.1).

Sustainability in outsourcing is new and relevant

Several senior executives commented that the sustainability factor in outsourcing was new, but they expected that sustainability would be a

Table 1.1   Seven reasons why sustainability is important in outsourcing

Reason
1 Sustainability in outsourcing is new and relevant to GITO
2 Sustainability will be driven by consumer concerns and employee expectations
3 Sustainability is important to an organization's brand reputation
4 Environmental topics are increasingly important sustainability issues
5 Due diligence is required to counter sustainability "greenwashing"
6 Government intervention forces sustainability capabilities
7 Emerging global sustainability standards will be applied to outsourcing providers

growing feature of outsourcing arrangements. A senior manager from IBM Canada stated, "Sustainability issues will not go away. They are complex and inter-related, across all business sectors." An advisor commented on a recent client request for an explicit sustainability profile in an outsourcing buyer Request for Proposal (RFP). In 2009, the Canada-based Centre for Outsourcing Research and Education (CORE) began to include a sustainability component in its education program for Accredited Outsourcing Practitioners. In 2009, the IAOP conducted its first survey of sustainability topics in order to provide guidance to its members. This survey was repeated in 2011, and the results are discussed below. The conclusion is that sustainability in outsourcing will continue to grow as an issue of importance.

Sustainability will be driven by consumer concerns and employee expectations

Many managers and advisors stressed the need to respond to consumer pressure for sustainable practices. Buyers commented that their organizations frequently responded to consumer pressures regarding sustainability issues, as demonstrated by the Nike case,[35] where consumers reacted negatively to the use of child labor in Nike supplier factories. Consumer product organizations have established sustainability frameworks and focus on products that may be tainted by sustainability issues such as the use of toxic materials or worker safety. Consumer-oriented organizations rely on international standards such as GRI to verify that suppliers are following appropriate sustainability standards. Reputation is an important issue in outsourcing, and sustainability practice is part of the building and protection of reputation.[36] Companies that have established sustainability processes for consumer products and services may be well equipped to quickly apply those methods to an outsourcing arrangement. For example, a GITO buyer in the retail sector told us of the need to review the ethical considerations in new merchandise offerings, such as labor conditions in manufacturing and the materials used to make the merchandise. These evaluation methods are also used to validate the sustainability of outsourcing providers.

Our research has shown the importance that managers give to their employees' perception of sustainability. The age of employees seemed to have a bearing in some firms where younger employees expressed high expectations of their employer's sustainability activity. This may become increasingly prominent as young employees replace the retiring "baby boom" generation. The implication is that employers, especially in

GITO providers (which often rely heavily on bright, young talent), need a strong and positive sustainability profile to attract and retain employees. Researchers at the Massachusetts Institute of Technology, USA, have come to similar conclusions.[37] One manager told us, "Sustainability is about retaining employees and nurturing new ones." A corollary of this is that outsourcing buyers and providers will need to communicate sustainability practices to relevant internal as well as external stakeholders. All of this underlines the need to identify, understand and monitor the sustainability expectations of key stakeholders such as consumers and employees, and to measure and report performance against these expectations.

Sustainability is important to an organization's brand reputation

Several managers at major outsourcing providers stated awareness of the need to protect their reputation and of the fact that sustainability practices play a role in that. Several managers mentioned how the offshore outsourcing centers of major firms looked identical to North American corporate campuses in terms of office layout, health and safety and equipment, providing assurance that workers were treated equally, even though salaries were lower than those paid in North America or Europe. A manager at the outsourcing provider Tata Consultancy Services stated that its sustainability abilities had become a definite advantage compared to competitors, especially when compared to second-tier, or start-up, outsourcing providers. Second-tier providers may be less attentive to their corporate reputation, and several managers told us that this may be a risk to a provider's sustainability reputation (see Chapter 3 for our analysis of the capabilities of providers). SRO (described above) encourages outsourcing to less well-established locales. Engagement in SRO may positively impact the reputation of a provider and possibly the outsourcing buyer.

Environmental topics are increasingly important sustainability issues

The government of British Columbia, Canada, now "requires an outsourcer to comply with government goals of 30% reduction in carbon [greenhouse gasses] output by 2020", according to a manager from EDS. The Canadian government requires outsourcing providers to supply "green" data centers, which can be challenging for providers who built data centers when power was relatively cheap. This concern was echoed by an executive from another GITO provider who said, "Sustainability issues will be driven by increasing costs of power and potential government carbon tax issues." *The Green IT Review*[38] has pointed to the impact of the United Kingdom's CRC on local and offshore data centers, suggesting that this cap-and-trade emissions reduction scheme will encourage more outsourcing of data centers and may penalize large UK-based data centers. At a 2008 IDC conference titled "GreenIT", the conference chair commented on how rapidly the topic of environmental responsibility had developed in the last two years. Furthermore, in 2010, the premier academic journal *MIS Quarterly* issued a call for papers to discuss the role of information systems in sustainability, with a focus on environmental issues.

For some outsourcing providers, attention to environmental responsibility will be both an economic issue and a reputational issue. Some providers see environmental responsibility as a competitive advantage in the outsourcing market. Environmentally friendly power may be driven by economic needs as the cost of power continues to rise, especially for data centers and related technology. For example, as power costs increase and power consumption in data centers increases, organizations must become more diligent in how they design and deploy ICT capabilities.

A key implication for IT infrastructure outsourcing providers will be the need for an efficient carbon management model. For example, although outsourcing a data center from North America to India may result in lower costs, it may also result in higher carbon emissions because of the use of power from "dirtier" sources such as diesel and coal. As organizations begin to report their environmental profiles to stakeholders, those profiles are likely to include IT outsourcing providers. These providers will be expected to be at least as carbon-efficient as their customers. Such reporting is already evident in the CDP,[39] which collects information from major global organizations to report carbon emissions from operations, including supply-chain and outsourcing providers. In 2008, 1,550 global organizations participated in the CDP, representing an estimated 26% of all global carbon emissions.

Due diligence is required to counter sustainability "greenwashing"

Several managers cautioned that sustainability could become a part of GITO providers' marketing messages. Outsourcing providers may quickly respond to consumer concerns with slick marketing messages rather than substantive sustainability programs. One manager described this as "corporate social responsibility hypocrisy". A thorough review of sustainability credentials in the due diligence phase of contracting is the best way to ensure that the provider can live up to the sustainability requirements of the buyer. A walk-through also protects against false sustainability claims or "greenwashing", where an organization presents an environmentally responsible public profile but lacks the actual sustainability policies and practices. However, standards or norms other than the buyer's own expectations for sustainability are not yet developed and widely used. Chapter 6 will explore this theme in more detail and describe the ethical review process that one company, Co-operative Financial Services (CFS), uses to validate sustainability capabilities in outsourcing providers.

Government intervention forces sustainability capabilities

Government policies to reduce carbon emissions, usually through a carbon tax, have forced outsourcing providers to become more efficient in power consumption while building IT infrastructure. In Canada, at least one province, British Colombia, has implemented a carbon tax, and others are discussing that possibility. Other jurisdictions, such as the state of California in the United States, have similar laws that impact how an organization manages its carbon footprint. In 2011, the Australian government introduced a plan for a carbon tax designed to reduce carbon emissions.[40] For IT infrastructure outsourcers, these government interventions indicate that efficient energy and carbon management capabilities are already important. For example, outsourcing a data center from North America to India may result in lower hard costs but may lead to higher carbon emissions because of the less efficient power sources. The implication here is for buyers to continue to be attentive to changing government regulations in all jurisdictions where the outsourcing provider and its buyers operate.

Emerging global sustainability standards will be applied to outsourcing providers

The International Organization for Standardization Working Group on Social Responsibility (sustainability) standard, ISO 26000, "provides guidance on the underlying principles of social responsibility, the core subjects and issues pertaining to social responsibility and on ways to implement social responsibility within an organization". These guidelines were accepted by ISO members in 2010 and the standards are about to become the global benchmark for sustainability across all organizations in all industries. Similarly, the GRI, which provides a uniform structure for reporting, is likely to emerge as a key standard for assessing GITO providers.

Table 1.2 presents the views of managers and researchers on the importance of sustainability to GITO. The managers interviewed were from a law firm based in Toronto, Canada; IBM Global Services; and Tata Consultancy Services. The academic researchers interviewed were from the Ryerson University Institute for the Study of Corporate Social Responsibility, Canada.

Table 1.2 Summary of managers' views on sustainability in outsourcing

Key theme	Quotes from managers
• CSR in outsourcing is new and relevant	• "CSR issues do not go away [with outsourcing]. They are complex and inter-related, across all business sectors." • "Every RFP has a sustainability component." • "CSR is about leading by example, not just philanthropy." • "CSR involves incorporating environmental and social impacts into all decisions made by a company [including outsourcing]."
• Sustainability will be driven by response to consumer concerns, which are enabled by global access to information through the Internet	• "The sustainability movement is Internet driven, allowing people around the world to come together on issues . . . stakeholders have become more empowered." • "Mobilization on the Internet and consumer demand/voice are driving the sustainability initiative." • "The Internet allows communication across borders, inexpensively. Lower barriers lead to increased trade (WTO, GATT) . . . You can trade, but a new set of questions arise . . . How are you operating there? [examples: China, India, mining companies] What is the social license?" • "Globalization has impacted sustainability by highlighting issues of labour standards"
• Due diligence is required to counter sustainability "greenwashing"	• "Where there are marketing opportunities, people will take them. Everybody has something to say about being green." • "Consider the halo effect . . . In a survey, 30% of respondents said they always think about the environment when making a purchase, but only 3% do at the register . . . Companies that talk the talk but don't walk the walk: Nike was caught in the 90s for being unable to deliver what they had promised . . . The first thing a company should do is 'Just Do It', and then you can talk about it." • "There is a delicate balance between saying nothing and saying too much about sustainability efforts."
• Global sustainability standards are being defined	• "It's a headache for global companies . . . Survey fatigue leads to coordinated disclosure to save energy answering questions." • "CSR depends on the business you are in . . . The Global Reporting Initiative opens the door to sustainability, driving change psychologically . . . The Equator Principles are used at banks for large loans . . . Sullivan Principles . . . Responsible Care Program for the chemical industry . . . ISO, the McDonald's of standards. The ISO 26000 for sustainability is being developed right now."

Sustainability in outsourcing: a view from the field

To understand the trends and key issues in sustainability and GITO, we collected data through three surveys involving three professional associations dedicated to outsourcing: CORE in Canada, the IAOP based in the United States and the NOA based in the United Kingdom.[41] The highlights of trends and issues we found are as follows:

1) **Due diligence gap.** There is a gap between buyer sustainability expectations and validation of provider sustainability credentials. Providers who are sustainability leaders may be able to influence buyers who have not fully established their sustainability requirements and validation processes. In our interviews, buyers told us that sustainability credentials were "table stakes" and expected that the providers would be able to demonstrate sustainability credentials. Similarly, we heard that although providers consistently described their sustainability credentials, buyers did not always assess or examine the provider's credentials. Overall, outsourcing providers appeared to be better prepared than were buyers regarding sustainability standards, with only 6% of providers unsure of which standards they participated in or subscribed to, while 24% of buyers were unsure. This supports our view that providers who are sustainability leaders may have an advantage in the competitive GITO market. This concept will be explored further in Chapter 3, where we measure the sustainability maturity of GITO providers, and in Chapter 4, where we describe how providers who are sustainability leaders can achieve competitive benefits through collaborative sustainability.

2) **Importance of sustainability to GITO.** Summary results from the three surveys are listed in Figure 1.3 in a chart that shows the decrease from the stated importance of sustainability (question 1) to the evaluation of the outsourcing provider (question 2) to the actual validation of sustainability credentials (question 3). The decrease in frequency of positive response from question 1 to 2 to 3 is consistent between NOA, CORE and IAOP surveys. About 87% of the NOA respondents in the United Kingdom stated that sustainability was important. Interestingly, although 66% of outsourcing buyers included sustainability requirements in their procurement processes, only 50% gave preference to outsourcing providers who demonstrated sustainability credentials. Canadian responses were similar to the UK responses. In a set of surveys from CORE, 95% of respondents agreed

Table 1.3   Survey summary – Sustainability in outsourcing

Question	NOA Survey n = 32 (%)	CORE Survey n = 44 (%)	IAOP Survey n = 166 (%)
How important is sustainability in outsourcing?	87	95	64
Consider sustainability in evaluation of outsourcing provider?	50	48	41
Validate provider sustainability credentials?	n/a	26	31
Would not consider outsourcing as a social responsibility	42	75	58

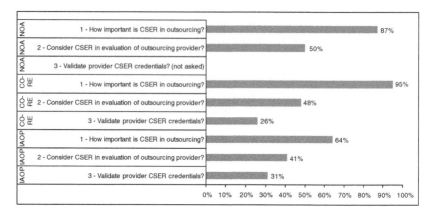

Figure 1.3   Comparing sustainability's stated importance with sustainability action
Source: IAOP, NOA, CORE, Authors' analysis.

that sustainability would be more important in future outsourcing contracts; 48% of Canadian buyers considered sustainability capabilities of the outsourcing provider when deciding to buy, compared to 50% in the United Kingdom. However, only 26% of Canadian outsourcing buyers validated provider sustainability capabilities. In Canada, 40% of buyers included sustainability requirements as part of the formal evaluation criteria. This demonstrates a consistency between the UK and Canadian GITO markets, which is repeated in the IAOP survey results. The results also demonstrate a gap between what buyers say and what they do, supporting our proposition of an opportunity for sustainability leaders. The largest survey was conducted by the IAOP.

The importance of sustainability in outsourcing was confirmed in this survey. Buyers reported that 30% of the time they always or often considered the sustainability ability of the provider when making an outsourcing decision. An additional 34% of buyers sometimes considered sustainability in an outsourcing decision; 41% of buyers always, often or sometimes evaluated the outsourcing provider's social responsibility capability as part of the formal outsourcing evaluation criteria. Similar to the UK and Canadian results, IAOP buyers were less likely to validate sustainability abilities, with only 31% of buyers ensuring that outsourcing providers complied with social and environmental standards, through internal or third-party audits of the outsourcing providers.

3) **SRO.** One final sustainability topic that was asked of NOA, CORE and IAOP members was related to SRO. In the IAOP survey, 58% of respondents revealed they never or rarely outsourced to developing regions of the world as SRO. In the NOA survey, 42% of respondents did not consider SRO. At CORE, 75% of respondents never or rarely outsourced to developing regions of the world as a social responsibility. As a result, we conclude that SRO is a niche activity. We note that rural sourcing, especially in the United States, is a type of SRO and appears to be increasing in some markets,[42] but broader data on global SRO is just beginning to become available.

Conclusion

The prominence of outsourcing and sustainability has emerged over the last 20 years. Both outsourcing and sustainability have become increasingly recognized, and the intersection of these two topics will become increasingly important both for buyers and for providers of outsourcing services in the future. However, today there is agreement regarding the importance of sustainability, active inclusion of sustainability requirements in RFPs, but relatively limited due diligence review and validation of provider sustainability credentials.

Appendix – About the Research

The research for this book was conducted in three phases. Phase 1 involved a series of qualitative interviews conducted over two years starting in mid-2008. In Phase 2, a set of surveys were used to collect responses from outsourcing professionals in IAOP, CORE and NOA, and there was an examination of the sustainability credentials on the outsourcing provider websites. Phase 3 involved the detailed case study at CFS, conducted in 2010 and completed in 2011.

Phase 1: Qualitative. April 2008–January 2010

Preliminary research fieldwork was conducted in 2008. The qualitative component consisted of semistructured interviews and a focus group. The interviewees were senior executives in their representative organizations, who were initially contacted to confirm their interest in this research topic.

A focus group discussion was conducted in late 2008, with four of the interviewees as panel members. The panel was sponsored by CORE and was conducted at Ryerson University, Canada, with an audience of approximately 50 persons. The focus group confirmed and elaborated on the themes identified by the initial interviews.

After the preliminary interviews, four exploratory pilot case studies were conducted. The cases involved a relatively small number of interviewees, ranging from two to seven per case. For the pilot cases, the researcher visited four organizations and conducted multiple interviews in person and on the phone, to discuss sustainability in outsourcing. Two sets of interviews were conducted with outsourcing buyers Enbridge Gas in Toronto and Rio Tinto in Montreal and their respective outsourcing providers, Tata Consultancy Services and Accenture. Follow-up discussions were conducted by telephone. Two sets of interviews were conducted with representatives from global IT outsourcing providers Accenture and a large Indian outsource provider. For Accenture, interviews were conducted at their offices in Toronto, Canada, and Bangalore, India. In addition to the interviews, several research reports from Accenture were reviewed. For a large Indian outsource provider interviews were conducted at their offices in India.

In the interviews, the focus group and the four pilot case studies the following topics were explored:

- When making outsourcing decisions, do evaluation criteria include sustainability capabilities?
- What components of sustainability, such as employee support, environmental stewardship, working environment, community involvement, etc., are most important?
- How do buyers give preference to sustainability factors in outsourcing decisions?
- Will sustainability considerations become more important in future outsourcing contracts?

Phase 2: Quantitative. June 2008–October 2010

The quantitative phase consisted of two methods. First, we conducted a series of surveys of outsourcing providers, buyers and advisors (e.g. lawyers, consultants). Second, we analyzed the content on outsourcing provider websites for sustainability references.

Surveys

CORE conducts a series of management training sessions to educate individuals on outsourcing management. After four sessions (seven days) of training, participants write a final exam and become Accredited Outsourcing Professionals (AOP). CORE includes a sustainability module within this training, and agreed to allow a paper-based survey to be collected from the class participants. The survey was voluntary and anonymous, although some participants voluntarily provided their name and email for follow-up discussion.

IAOP agreed to conduct a similar electronic survey of its members regarding sustainability in 2009. The survey was much broader than the CORE survey and was conducted using IAOP's proprietary electronic survey tool. The IAOP survey was announced through an email in late July 2009 to several thousand IAOP members and affiliates. In total, 178 responses had been received by the end of November 2009. Half of the responses came from outsourcing providers. Of the remaining respondents, 29% were outsourcing buyers and 17% were advisors. The final 4% were academic and press representatives. IAOP repeated this survey in 2011 and plans to release the analysis in late-2012.

NOA conducted a similar survey, again with six questions that were aligned with both the CORE and IAOP surveys. The survey was distributed electronically to NOA members, and the results were collected in March and April 2010. A total of 53 surveys were collected. Table A.1 summarizes the survey data collected from all three sources.

Website content analysis

In the second component of the quantitative phase, we examined the content of websites of leading global outsourcing providers to understand how they publically present their sustainability credentials. We used the IAOP list of "2008 Global Outsourcing 100" to identify a list of 19 leading global IT outsourcing providers. We then examined the providers' websites to assess whether they participated in any of the global sustainability standards.

Table A.1   Summary of sustainability survey data collection

Data collection period	Source	Respondent location	Number of respondents	Comments
June 2008–October 2010	CORE	Canada	49	Paper survey distributed at training seminars
July 2009–November 2009	IAOP	Global, with 49% from USA	178	Proprietary IAOP electronic survey
March 2010–April 2010	NOA	UK	53	Proprietary NOA electronic survey
		Total responses	280	

Coding was conducted during May and June of 2009 by examining the provider website for any mention of the sustainability criteria established above. When a sustainability criterion was mentioned, the provider reference was cross-checked with the standards organization of the auditing organization for verification (e.g. GRI, CDP, ISO, UN). We determined an overall sustainability maturity as the arithmetic summation of whether the outsourcing provider participated in GRI, GRI verification, CDP, UN Global Compact, ISO 14001 and ISO 26000 and was listed in at least one Social Responsibility Index. To determine sustainability maturity, one point was allocated for participation in each of the above standards.

Phase 3: Qualitative. December 2009–January 2011

The final stage of the research was a detailed case study at Co-Operative Financial Services in Manchester, UK. The case interviews included representatives from the CFS outsourcing provider Steria. The case study was sponsored by the leader of the IT Strategic Partnerships Group, which is responsible for management of all IT outsourcing contracts with over 100 vendors. The Chief Information Officer at CFS strongly supported the case study, both as a participant and as a recipient of the final report. We interviewed the CIO in June 2010 and January 2011, and he commented on the importance and relevance of the research and his receptiveness to the emerging conceptual framework.

The case study was explanatory, seeking to explain new outsourcing models and business frameworks. In selecting CFS as our case study, we found an organization with a very strong social commitment, which allows this research to create a model as a guide to other organizations. Moreover, the organization Steria has similar commitment to social responsibility, both locally and in India. By conducting interviews on-site at CFS over several weeks, in meeting rooms, in offices and in common areas such as the cafeteria, we gained a strong understanding of the culture and dynamics of the organization, which could not have been gleaned through other research methods such as a survey or a focus group. For example, we learned about the strong social responsibility of CFS by reading their newsletters and postings. We learned of the importance of measuring their progress holistically, with the IS-balanced scorecard posted throughout the Information Systems department.

The phenomenon of sustainability in outsourcing was not frequently discussed when we began our research in 2008, and the real-life context of CFS provided strong evidence of contemporary practices to which theoretical frameworks can be added to create a model for others to emulate. CFS as a member of the co-operative group has a very strong social orientation that began in 1844. The outsourcing provider Steria also has a strong social orientation. Although there may be other examples of outsourcing buyers and providers with strong social orientations, this case provided an exemplary model for examination of sustainability in outsourcing.

The case study consisted of four stages.

The first stage involved initial contact between the research team and CFS. During this stage, the credibility of the research team was established as well as the terms of reference for the study and the discussion outline for the interviews. The first stage began in December 2009 and was completed by May 2010. Two face-to-face meetings were conducted in December 2009 and January 2010 during the first stage, with the case sponsor in Manchester.

The second stage was an intensive two-week period of interviews conducted on-site at CFS headquarters in Manchester, UK, in June and July 2010. In this period, 23 interviews were completed. Most interviews were conducted in a conference room at CFS. When the conference room was unavailable, interviews were conducted in the CFS cafeteria.

The third stage, which was conducted after the initial analysis, involved secondary field work, reviewing the preliminary findings and collecting further data. Additional documents identified in the interviews were collected and reviewed. Five follow-up interviews were conducted to gather additional information that may have been missed in the first round. This stage was completed in January 2011.

The fourth and final stage of the CFS case study consisted of the sharing of information with key stakeholders in the case study, for discussion and, if appropriate, for planning purposes. A management report was presented to the CFS executives, the CIO and the head of the IT outsourcing unit. This allowed the researcher to validate initial interview findings, to explore the concepts developed in the interviews, to develop an emerging theoretical model with the executives and to continue to build trust and support for the research. Both executives were very receptive to the interpretation of findings and the implications for their operations. We also conducted additional interviews with Steria executives and presented our preliminary findings for discussion. In addition, the research findings were presented and discussed at an NOA seminar in Manchester in January 2011. The seminar was attended by about 40 people. At the seminar, presentations on sustainability and social responsibility were also delivered by The National Trust, Fujitsu, Cadburys, the Centre for Development Informatics and by the host, legal firm DWF.

2
Integrating Sustainability and Outsourcing

Corporate social responsibility is about leading by example, not just philanthropy.

Development Lead, Tata Consultancy Services

Sustainability involves incorporating environmental and social impacts into all decisions made by a company [including outsourcing]. Companies now have to be aware of the claim of hypocrisy – being good at home, but bad abroad...CSR is about the rules you should follow, as the law only goes so far.

Dr. Kernaghan Webb, Director, Institute for the
Study of CSR, Ryerson University

Introduction

Our research has tracked the evolution of sustainability into outsourcing arrangements since 2005. We have observed the increasing importance given to sustainability issues by buyers who demand that their providers are able to match the standards through the outsourcing supply chain.

This chapter asks the question: how are buyers and providers incorporating sustainability into outsourcing relationships?

On the basis of the research undertaken between 2008 and 2010, this chapter reports the findings from studying how organizations are incorporating sustainability into relationships and in some cases collaborating. This chapter identifies the step changes that buyers and providers have taken to incorporate sustainability into outsourcing relationships and the processes and practices on which it should be based.

In this chapter, we study two relationships selected for the client's outsourcing experience and relative maturity in dealing with sustainability

issues in their domain. We also report on the views of experienced practitioners, including senior executives in provider firms, consultants and
lawyers, about the outsourcing sustainability models benefits and practices.

The chapter proceeds first by giving details of two cases focusing on how
sustainability was incorporated into the outsourcing arrangement. We then
describe a framework for incorporating sustainability into outsourcing relationships with lessons for both buyers and providers. Throughout the
chapter, we provide examples drawn from recent research.

Incorporating sustainability into outsourcing: Emerging models

We noted in our research that there were organizations leading the way
toward incorporating sustainability into outsourcing with providers. The
first case study presented below is from our study of Enbridge Gas Distribution in Toronto, Canada, where both IT and business processes were
outsourced to two global outsourcing providers, Accenture and TCS. The
second case study is from our study at Rio Tinto mining in Montréal,
Canada, where once again both IT and business process services were
outsourced to Accenture and CGI. The two case studies provide several
blueprints of practices they were working on, in particular the standards,
and processes such as balanced scorecard measurements and importance of
aligned values between buyer and provider, the "cultural fit".

Case 2.1: A gas company's integration of sustainability with its provider

Enbridge provides an interesting case study because of its prominent public sustainability profile and very extensive engagement in IT outsourcing
over the last ten years. Enbridge Gas Distribution is a business unit of
Enbridge Inc., a larger publically traded corporation. Enbridge Gas Distribution represents 16% of the overall Enbridge Inc. corporate earnings for
the year 2010.[1] Enbridge has three currently active outsourcing contracts.
The contracts are long-term (one is for ten years, another is for a five-year
term) and of significant value. The company outsources its customer service business operations, enterprise system (SAP) support and additional
staff skills. All outsourcing decisions are reviewed by the executive management team (EMT), and the director of public, government and aboriginal
affairs is a member of that team. When outsourcing decisions are made,
sustainability is not an explicit evaluation criterion, but the director of

public, government and aboriginal affairs stated: "we should probably raise that" with outsourcing providers. Regarding sustainability expectations for outsourcing providers, the Enbridge IT director stated: "we evaluate cultural fit", and after the RFP response is reviewed, "it becomes important to understand cultural fit" of the provider.

Enbridge has taken steps to understand and document its complete carbon footprint. It measured a baseline in 2009 and rollout of a complete carbon data management system in 2010. Enbridge participates in the GRI and the CDP, and the organization's CEO has "committed to being carbon neutral by 2015". The organization publishes an annual CSR report that is based on GRI reporting requirements; the Enbridge report for 2008 was of 55 pages and the 2010 report was of 190 pages, reflecting a growing commitment to sustainability and increased communication with stakeholders.

The director of public, government and aboriginal affairs stated that Enbridge "does not ask outsourcers" to participate in CDP and GRI, although the EMT reviews all proposed outsourcing contracts to understand "the balance of cost savings versus impact to the Enbridge brand and image". The Director further commented that although sustainability concerns at Enbridge are increasing, the company is in the early stages of its commitment to sustainable outsourcing. The organization is implementing a new metric in the balanced scorecard to measure "brand and corporate responsibility", which will be rated for all employees and "will have an impact on [personal] compensation".

The director of public, government and aboriginal affairs stated that Enbridge prides itself on "brand and trust of environmental responsibility". Sustainability is seen as a valuable organizational characteristic because of the "reputation that brings and retains customers". In addition, "younger employees demand it. We are looked on as leaders, and there is so much more to do."

Regarding outsourcing evaluations, the director of IT stated that Enbridge can "see sustainability becoming increasingly important in the future".

Enbridge outsources to TCS for the IT staff augmentation services. The partnership provides "an extension of knowledge, reduced costs and improved quality". Improved quality comes from a higher level of methodology rigor, for example using capability maturity model (CMM) level 5 for software design and development.

Enbridge neither formally specified sustainability capability in its RFPs nor did it specify any environmental requirements. However, TCS has a strong profile on sustainability issues throughout the global Tata Corporation, whose mission statement insists that "TCS must have an impact on the community that it is part of."

TCS has committed to work with Enbridge to develop balanced scorecard reporting and measurement to help focus on environmental responsibility, taking a holistic view of the overall Enbridge IT operation. The emphasis will be on "simplification, process orchestration and virtualization" and on "data center server reduction". These measures are not yet "baked into" the balanced scorecard but will be introduced in 2012, as both Enbridge and TCS "co-embrace" these environmental responsibility issues. The interviewee stated that these issues are "not sales tools" but are fundamental to the outsourcing business.

The TCS country manager emphasized that TCS has committed to sustainability at the corporate level, with a chief sustainability officer who works with account teams to support causes that are important to clients. TCS reports an achieved "2% reduction in the carbon footprint in FY 07-08 compared to the prior year". TCS will conduct a sustainability project "in conjunction with clients where the outcome can be measured in a meaningful way". The primary objective of the current outsourcing relationship with Enbridge "is to deliver on all parameters", and then "take it to the second level. When sustainability becomes a measurement point in one to two years, that will represent a maturity in the relationship" with Enbridge.

TCS appears to anticipate growing sustainability expectations from buyers, such as Enbridge, which are aligned with the growth of sustainability in outsourcing identified in Chapter 1.

The Enbridge–TCS case suggests the importance of sustainability in developing the outsourcing relationship to greater levels of maturity. Outsourcing providers, especially global organizations such as TCS, have recognized that buyers expect leadership in social and environmental responsibility. For example, the "cultural fit" requirement articulated by executives at Enbridge suggests that providers must align with the sustainability profile of their buyers. If sustainability is important for a buyer such as Enbridge, then providers such as TCS must fit with that expectation. The outsourcing provider's sustainability reputation must reinforce and not detract from the buyer's. For example, reduced energy consumption, which results in lower carbon emissions, is good for business because it also lowers operating costs. Saving money through more efficient power consumption in data centers will always be an attractive business proposition from outsourcing providers to their buyers. Outsourcing providers recognize this; for example, Accenture has advocated green data centers[2] and the environmental benefits of moving to cloud computing.[3] Outsourcing providers gain additional advantage when cost savings are also seen as environmentally responsible, helping to improve the "green" brand and image of the provider and its clients.

Although sustainability was not a formal evaluation criterion in the Enbridge RFP, when Enbridge executives conducted a site review as part of the final RFP assessment, the sustainability component later became a qualifying criterion. Sustainability may not have won the competition for TCS, but lack of sustainability capability could have lost the competition, due to poor "cultural fit". After winning the outsourcing bid, sustainability capability is expected as part of the overall partnership and will be gradually introduced as a balanced scorecard measurement. Standards such as GRI, CDP and the UN Global Compact will inform inputs to the measurement.

Learning points

- Buyers look for sustainability as part of the "cultural fit" of an outsourcing provider.
- Outsourcing providers are working to develop more efficient power consumption, to reduce costs and to appear to be more environmentally responsible.
- Sustainability will not be the deciding factor for buyers in awarding outsourcing contracts to providers, but lack of capability could reduce an outsourcing provider's qualifications in a bidding competition.
- Global sustainability standards can be used by buyers to assess provider capabilities and to quantify cultural fit.

Case 2.2: Sustainability and outsourcing at a global mining firm

Rio Tinto is a global mining and metals processing firm. Major products include aluminum, copper, diamonds, energy products, industrial minerals and iron ore. As a mining firm, Rio Tinto has a very direct environmental impact and thus has long-established policies and practices regarding environmental sustainability. In 2008, Rio Tinto published a statement of business practices entitled "The Way We Work".[4] This document addresses openness and accountability as well as corporate policies regarding the environment, human rights, occupational health and safety and sustainable development. Rio Tinto has signed the UN Global Compact and supports many international social responsibility accords. A second Rio Tinto document called "The Way We Buy"[5] is a statement of procurement policies and practices within the organization. This document defines how Rio Tinto will engage with suppliers and what the organization expects of its suppliers. Rio Tinto expects that its suppliers will comply with all the standards set out in "The Way We Work", thus encouraging suppliers to adopt the same sustainability standards that Rio Tinto applies to itself.

Rio Tinto is divided into multiple business units depending on the line of business. Interviews for this research were conducted at the Rio Tinto Aluminum (RTA) business unit, which is based in Montréal. This business unit was formerly known as Alcan (the Aluminum Company of Canada).

Rio Tinto's sustainability focus is twofold. First, it concentrates on health, safety and environment (HSE). Second, it focuses on community relations. Rio Tinto's director of sustainable development and community relations in Montréal identified a global community relations diagnostic that Rio Tinto uses to self-assess its global sustainability. The results from the diagnostic are recorded in a global social environmental working tool. The process is reviewed by external auditor PricewaterhouseCoopers. The director noted that sustainability is viewed as a competitive advantage by Rio Tinto. He told us the following:

- Much of Rio Tinto's resource development occurs in non-Organisation for Economic Co-operation and Development countries, which generally have less developed social and environmental abilities. For example, in Madagascar a new site is being developed that is expected to remain active for more than 60 years. Forty-five percent of the labor force must be imported from elsewhere because of inadequate local skills. Rio Tinto has committed to educational investment in the local population, with the expectation of lowering its labor costs over the 60-year life of the site.
- Malaria is prevalent in Africa where Rio has and plans to develop many sites. Malaria creates labor force absenteeism, for either the individual worker or when the worker must care for a sick family member. The company's investment in community malaria prevention helps to decrease labor costs through improved attendance.
- HSE and community activities are considered not only from a social perspective but are also run through a financial model, so that appropriate investments are made in the short term for long-term benefit at Rio Tinto.

Most of Rio Tinto's IT operations are outsourced. Each business unit operates its own information systems and technology (IS&T). Global IS&T provides a set of shared services and IT capabilities for all business units.

For example, Global IS&T delivers an SAP application that supports 25,000 business users. Global software application support for SAP is outsourced to a large Indian GITO provider. Computer Science Corporation (CSC) provides IT infrastructure support to all Rio Tinto global business units. At RTA, local IT infrastructure support has been outsourced to CGI, a Canada-based GITO provider. RTA has outsourced support for SAP software to global outsourcing provider Accenture.

Regarding sustainability considerations in outsourcing, the vice president of IS&T at RTA noted that the issue has become increasingly important over the last eight years:

- in 2001, when the Alcan data center was outsourced to CGI, sustainability issues were not considered in the outsourcing arrangement;
- in 2006, when SAP support was outsourced to Accenture, there was considerable review of social responsibilities, which consisted of visits to Bangalore, India, to review employee support, well-being and skills development; and
- in a 2009 RFP for outsourcing software applications support, HSE considerations were part of the vendor evaluation criteria. This became a pattern for all future outsourcing contracts.

The superintendent for RTA North America procurement commented on the importance of "compliance with RT standards for sustainability" as part of the evaluation criteria for IT outsourcing. Providers are evaluated for their ability to deliver and to comply with RT standards prior to the award of an outsourcing contract. For example, RTA has checked the credentials of an outsourcing provider by going to the work site in Bangalore to audit the treatment of the workers and confirm compliance with RTA labor standards. Citing a recent procurement competition between IBM and HP, he commented, "price is not the only criteria, especially if the difference is marginal. Cultural fit with the values we share is very important because often outsource prices are comparable." He noted that sustainability will become more important in future procurements and he can see that trend "happening now". To illustrate, the following is an extract of a sustainability requirement from a recent RFP Rio Tinto sent to several major GITO providers in North America:

The Company is committed to the highest standards of safety, health and environmental practices and expects its suppliers to be similarly focused.... The company will seek to establish a relationship with a supplier that can demonstrate it has the appropriate health, safety and environmental objectives and has the management systems in place to deliver on these objectives.

Clearly the sustainability expectations at Rio Tinto have grown from initial outsourcing arrangements in 2001, and sustainability qualifications have become important for outsourcing providers in competitive RFPs.

Learning points

- Buyers look for cultural fit of an outsourcing provider, which includes sustainability profile. It is interesting to note that Rio Tinto's view of "cultural fit" mirrors Enbridge's expectations for outsourcing providers.
- Rio Tinto expects its suppliers to adopt the same sustainability standards that it applies, for example in the areas of HSE. This is another example for the importance of aligned values.
- The integration of sustainability expectations into relationships with outsourcing providers is growing and will distinguish providers where price and quality for products or services are comparable.

Integrating sustainability into outsourcing: The framework for success

Our case studies make very clear the success factors that are driving the incorporation of sustainability into outsourcing relationships. In the rest of the chapter, we consolidate this learning into five lessons for buyers and providers of outsourcing to incorporate sustainability. These are related to understanding regulations and standards, anticipating expectations, responding to inquiries, embedding sustainability into operations and developing a sustainability culture. Let's look at each of these in turn.

Lesson 1: Understand relevant sustainability regulatory requirements

GITO requires both buyers and providers to be aware of government and non-governmental organization standards and regulations. They require knowledge of relevant regulations and capabilities to apply them in an outsourcing arrangement. When specifying outsourcing requirements, usually in an RFP, buyers should refer to regulatory and legal sustainability requirements in the jurisdictions in which the buyer operates. Outsourcing requirements should provide information about the buyer's sustainability standards and expectations. For example, one buyer asks outsourcing providers to outline how they will comply with the social and environmental policies described on the buying organization's website. Buyers must also be able to assess a provider's sustainability credentials, through both an initial walk-through validation and ongoing confirmations. If buyer and provider have both agreed to adopt a global sustainability standard, such as GRI or ISO, compliance may be verified by an external party – for example, ongoing certification by the standards organization or by a third-party auditor.

GITO providers will need to understand and comply with global, regional and national sustainability regulations and statutory requirements. They should understand the current and emerging requirements in all jurisdictions where they, and their clients, operate. Providers that can provide leadership in this area may have an advantage over competing outsourcing providers that have less mature sustainability capability. Outsourcing providers with mature sustainability processes and practices will be able to provide leadership to their customers, especially when the provider's maturity is superior to that of the buying organization.

Lesson 2: Anticipate stakeholder sustainability expectations

Employees and customers increasingly influence sustainability requirements, implying that organizations must anticipate their expectations. They need the ability to monitor and manage stakeholder sustainability expectations. Anticipating these expectations allows organizations to readily respond to sustainability inquiries, as described in the third guideline below.

Buyers need a reporting capability to deliver to interested stakeholders information on sustainability performance and compliance with relevant laws, regulations and guidelines. They need to work with their outsourcing providers to build this reporting capability, since some or all of the data likely come from providers' operations. An example is the carbon management database at Enbridge that reports on organization-wide emissions; this database will be extended to include outsourcing provider information. Many large organizations already prepare an annual public report on sustainability performance. Increasingly, stakeholders will expect outsourcing provider information to be included in such reporting.

Providers should work closely with buyers to provide sustainability measures that meet global quality standards. Providers will need to measure and report on how they support the sustainability performance of individual clients.

Lesson 3: Respond to sustainability inquiries

Honest and forthright communication will increasingly be needed to confront the widespread skepticism on sustainability performance issues. Both outsourcing buyers and providers should expect inquiries from stakeholders, including government regulators, customers, news media, NGOs, shareholders, unions and employees, and must be able to respond.

Buyers should be trained in capturing, analyzing and responding to sustainability inquiries that will include requests for information about outsourcing arrangements.

Providers will need to work closely with outsourcing buyers to provide accurate and timely responses to inquiries. The ability of a provider to respond will reflect directly on the buyer's external reputation. In anticipation of inquiries, providers should work with buyers to prepare an information repository of client-specific sustainability information. The work of TCS to co-develop a sustainability scorecard with Enbridge is an example of this guideline put into action.

Lesson 4: Embed sustainability in ongoing operations

Our research shows that sustainability is not a short-term or in a transitory phase, as demonstrated by growing sustainability interest from the IAOP surveys shown in Chapter 1. The challenges of social and environmental issues, along with developing global standards, will require organizations to embed sustainability capabilities into their ongoing operations. To achieve this, they should be able to regularly update the sustainability knowledge base and to deploy that knowledge throughout the organization. Acquiring the necessary capabilities means hiring new people and training existing employees, as described in the fifth guideline below.

Buyers should build sustainability performance measures into outsourcing governance, using service-level agreements and other contractual mechanisms. Experts from within the buyer organization or from external advisory firms should define how outsourcing providers will support sustainability. Buyers should expect to provide regular outsourcing sustainability reports, such as a GRI report, to their stakeholders both within and outside of the organization.

Providers should adopt best practices that will help their clients improve their sustainability reporting. They should also offer clients a reporting process that will dovetail with and support clients' requirements

Table 2.1   Sustainability guidelines for GITO

Sustainability guideline	Implications for buyers	Implications for providers
1. Understand relevant regulatory requirements		
Understand regulatory and legal requirements for the client jurisdiction being served.	Articulate jurisdiction requirements to outsourcing providers through request for proposal and outsourcing governance processes.	Respond to various global, regional and national regulations and statutory requirements.
Understand industry-specific requirements (e.g. manufacturing, resources).	Validate outsourcing provider's ability to respond to regulatory and legal requirements, through audit and due diligence.	Demonstrate levels of compliance that are comparable to highest international standards through benchmarking against industry leaders.
Understand outsourcing-specific requirements (e.g. data center efficiency requirements).		
2. Anticipate stakeholder expectations		
Monitor and understand expectations of key stakeholder groups (e.g. employees, recruits, customers).	Working with the outsourcing provider, create factual reports on accomplishments and comparison to benchmarks and standards.	Provide global quality measures, according to international standards, that provide evidence of capability.
Communicate effectively and proactively with key stakeholder groups.	Communicate directly with key stakeholders. For example, provide a report to shareholders.	Measure and report on how individual client performance is being supported.
3. Respond to inquiries		
Provide factual information as requested by the government and other stakeholder groups.	Maintain a repository of information, including outsourcing providers' data.	Create client-specific sustainability information repositories.
	Respond to information requests.	Respond to client information requests.
4. Embed sustainability in ongoing operations		
Measure, compare, report and communicate accomplishments.	Establish sustainability programs as part of outsourcing management and governance.	Transfer best practices to clients.
	Use outside experts to define program.	Implement measurement and reporting processes that dovetail with client sustainability requirements.
	Communicate achievements proactively to stakeholder groups.	
5. Develop a sustainability culture through hiring and education		
Include sustainability skills in recruiting and hiring processes.	Emphasize the importance of skills for professional growth and success within the organization.	Recognize relative importance of skills within client organizations.
Create skill development opportunities within and outside of organization.	When recruiting, demonstrate importance of sustainability within the organizational culture.	Provide skill development opportunities and training to client organizations.

Source: Babin, R. and B. Nicholson (2009). "Corporate Social and Environmental Responsibility in Global IT Outsourcing." MIS Quarterly Executive 8(4): 123–132.

and obligations, which is what TCS is doing with balanced scorecard measurements at Enbridge Gas.

Lesson 5: Develop a sustainability culture through hiring and education

As described in the fourth guideline, sustainability is a long-term commitment for both GITO buyers and providers. Organizations will need an ongoing hiring and education program that builds a culture of social and environmental responsibility. The required skills will be focused on assessing and reinforcing sustainability concepts in the organization and its business partners. Professional organizations IAOP and CORE have included sustainability in their accreditation programs. Literature in management as well as our own has shown that organizations with a positive sustainability profile will be more successful in attracting and retaining promising young talent.

Both buyers and providers will need to continually develop their internal sustainability culture through hiring and education. Buyers will respond to the sustainability demands of their industry. Providers can become centers of excellence and provide sustainability guidance to their clients (Table 2.1).

Conclusion

All indications are that sustainability is growing as an important issue in the GITO industry. However, relatively few buyers are actively measuring sustainability credentials in their providers, and currently there are no sustainability standards for GITO. The set of guidelines for buyers and providers to develop sustainability within their organizations and in partnership with one another provides a relatively simple tool that facilitates management of the sustainability component of the deal. This forces the parties to consider the various dimensions of sustainability, think about and agree how they will work together at all stages of their relationship, from the RFP to provider selection to the ongoing operation of the relationship.

3
Measuring Sustainability

Clearly one of the topics that is looming large is understanding the kind of power consumption footprints of different choices.

M. Ellison, IT Strategy Leader, Co-operative Financial Services

Efforts to find shared value in operating practices and in the social dimensions of competitive context have the potential not only to foster economic and social development but to change the way companies and society think about each other.

Michael Porter and Mark Kramer, Harvard University

We recognize that there are physical limits to the resources of the Earth and that any business activity that exceeds such limits is by definition unsustainable and will need to be reconstituted. Furthermore, there are ethical and social components to sustainable development for which business should be accountable. These extend far beyond legislative compliance.

Co-operative Sustainable Procurement and Supplier Policy, applied to all outsourcing contracts

Introduction

In this chapter, we examine sustainable global outsourcing through the lens of GITO providers. The chapter begins with an examination of a set of 19 leading GITO providers to understand their sustainability maturity. We then describe two case studies, of outsourcing providers Accenture and a large Indian GITO provider, which seek to understand how these two providers apply sustainability concepts in their business operations. The chapter continues with presentation of the Sustainable Global Outsourcing model, a new model that applies directly to the outsourcing relationship between buyer and provider and describes how the relationship can be improved while also creating benefits for society and the environment. The model and this chapter provide guidance to outsourcing buyers and providers on how to measure and improve their sustainability in the outsourcing relationship.

Understanding sustainability maturity at global IT outsourcing providers

Our research examined the profile of leading global outsourcing providers, using content analysis to understand how they publically present their sustainability capabilities.

We used the IAOP list of top global outsourcing providers and focused on the leading IT outsourcing providers.[1] Table 3.1 provides the analysis of the top 19 outsourcing providers and correspondence to instances where interviews have also been undertaken. The overall sustainability maturity is an arithmetic summation of whether the outsourcing company participated in GRI, GRI verification, CDP, UN Global Compact, ISO 14001 and ISO 26000 and was listed in at least one socially responsible investment index. One point was allocated for participation in each of the above standards.

This analysis covered 19 representative, albeit large, GITO providers. A limitation of this research approach was that data and interviews for large GITO providers were readily available, whereas smaller providers were difficult to contact and sustainability data was not readily accessible.

Stages of sustainability in global IT outsourcing

Using the sustainability profiles from the content analysis phase, we plotted the scores of the 19 GITO providers, depicted in Figure 3.1. An "S" curve is drawn over the plot to represent the stages of growth. Analyzing the sustainability scores plotted in Figure 3.1, and with an understanding of the qualitative assessments provided from the interviews, we formulated a three-stage model. None of the providers attained a top score of 7, although five companies attained a score of 6. The top-scoring companies, with scores of 5 and 6, are deemed to be mature sustainability leaders. Companies with a score of 2, 3 or 4 are described as aspiring sustainability leaders, because they reported adoption of some but not all of the sustainability standards. Companies with a score of 0 or 1 are described as early stage sustainability adopters.

Table 3.1 Sustainability profile of top GITO providers

Company	IAOP 2008 Level	GRI	GRI verification	CDP	UN global compact (Join Date)	ISO 14001	ISO 26000	Indices	Overall sustainability maturity
Accenture	1	2008 Spain	GRI	2007–2008	2008	Yes	–	DJSI NA, FTSE4Good	6
IBM Global Services	2	2007–2008	Self	2003–2008	–	Yes	–	DJSI NA/World	5
Infosys	3	2008	GRI/DNV	2006–2008	2001	Yes	–	S&P ESG	6
Capgemini	5	–	–	2006–2008	2004	Intention	–	FTSE4Good	4
TCS	6	2007–2008	GRI	2008	2006	Yes	–	S&P ESG, DJSI World	6
WiPro	7	2009	DNV	2007–2008	2008	Yes	–	S&P ESG	6
HP	8	2002–2008	Bureau Veritas	2003–2008	2002	Yes	–	DJSI NA/World, FTSE4Good	6
Genpact	9	–	–	–	–	Yes	–	–	1
Tech Mahindra	10	2008	GRI, Ernst & Young	–	2001	–	–	S&P ESG	4
HCL Technologies	11	–	–	–	–	Yes	–	–	1
EDS	12	2008	Self	2007–2008	–	Yes	Intention	–	4
ACS	13	–	–	–	–	–	–	–	0

50

Table 3.1 (Continued)

Company	IAOP 2008 Level	GRI	GRI verification	CDP	UN global compact (Join Date)	ISO 14001	ISO 26000	Indices	Overall sustainability maturity
CGI	14	–	–	2006–2008	–	–	–	FTSE4Good	2
HOV Services	15	–	–	–	–	–	–	–	0
Mastek	16	–	–	–	–	–	–	–	0
Hexaware	22	–	–	–	–	–	–	–	0
CSC	23	–	–	–	2008	Yes	–	–	2
Unisys	24	–	–	2006–2008	–	Yes	–	–	2
Atos Origin	n/a	–	–	2007–2008	–	Intention	–	–	2

Source: Babin and Nicholson (2011).

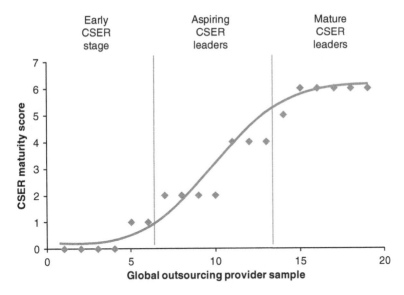

Figure 3.1 Sustainability maturity of GITO providers
Source: Adapted from Babin and Nicholson (2011, p. 57).

This stage model is similar to the stage models presented by other researchers.[2] Richard Nolan is widely credited with introducing the concept of stages of growth to the management of computer resources more than 35 years ago. Nolan's stages-of-growth model predicts the change of IT focus from cost reduction in accounting applications (stage 1) to integrated information management through database applications (stage 4). The model allows organizations to predict different goals and management expectations for IT resources at different stages. The success and durability of the stages model can be seen in the continuing academic research and practitioner discussion since Nolan's first articles.[3]

These concepts will be used later in this chapter to describe how outsourcing providers can move from early stages of sustainability, with appropriate groundwork, to more mature sustainability stages.[4]

In addition, the stages-of-growth model has been applied to various business areas. Recently, Nidumolu et al.[5] have described five stages for using sustainability as a key driver for innovation and growth. In the specific domain of GITO, Carmel and Agarwal suggest that "offshore IT sourcing follows a stages model, based on increasing maturity and sophistication in the offshore effort". The Carmel and Agarwal model can be used by IT executives to benchmark activities and understand how "to leverage offshore resources in delivering their IT solutions". We draw on the stages of growth approach as it offers a robust means to identify, classify and assess sustainability maturity in outsourcing. This presents a means for practical assessment of an outsourcing providers' stage of sustainability maturity and enables planning for the next stage of sustainability growth. In addition, the stages-of-growth model is used to understand the progression of trust in an outsourcing relationship, from early stages to more mature levels, which will be used to explain collaborative sustainability in the next chapter.

The stages-of-growth model can be useful in identifying actions required to move to the next level of maturity. The stage model described below is a new contribution to outsourcing practitioners that will guide them on how and when to further develop sustainability, based on their current sustainability maturity. For example, those in early stages should focus on one or two of the sustainability standards, such as preparing an annual sustainability report using GRI guidance.

In addition to the sustainability maturity scores, interviews with buyers and providers provided detail on the sustainability maturity in relation to three capability characteristics:

1) the ability to understand and adopt global sustainability standards;
2) the ability to anticipate and respond to sustainability requests from stakeholders; and
3) the ability to embed and develop sustainability capabilities within the organization through hiring and ongoing training.

Three stages of maturity

Below we describe the characteristics of each stage of sustainability maturity.

Stage 3: Mature Sustainability Leaders: The highest level of maturity contains the GITO sustainability leaders who have adopted and participated in global environmental standards. The mature leaders are listed in one or more social responsibility index, such as the Financial Times Stock Exchange for Good (FTSE-4-Good). These leaders establish the sustainability benchmarks for the GITO industry. The leaders provide valued consulting advice to their customers on sustainability.

Stage 2: Aspiring Sustainability Leaders: At the next level of maturity, GITO providers participated in some of the global standards or stated an intention to participate. These providers aspire to global sustainability and follow the lead of the more mature organizations.

Stage 1: Early Stage Sustainability: In the early stage of sustainability, GITO providers have not yet embraced sustainability, or have decided that sustainability is not important or not affordable.

Table 3.2 summarizes how these three characteristics are displayed in the three stages of sustainability maturity in GITO providers.

Table 3.2   Key sustainability characteristics for GITO providers

	Mature sustainability leaders	Aspiring sustainability leaders	Early stages of sustainability maturity
1) Understand and adopt global sustainability standards	• Participate in all of GRI, CDP, ISO 14000 and ISO 26000, UN Global Compact • Strong executive commitment to sustainability standards	• Participate in some of GRI, CDP, ISO 14000 and ISO 26000, UN Global Compact • Stated intention to increase participation in sustainability standards	• No participation in global sustainability standards • Examples of sustainability projects but lacking certification
2) Anticipate and respond to stakeholder sustainability requests	• Protocol and responsibility established for stakeholder sustainability communication • Increasing volume of white papers on sustainability • Growing sustainability consulting practice • Regular public reporting of sustainability performance	• General responses through prepared environmental statements, not customized to individual stakeholder groups or issues	• No formal public reporting of sustainability performance • Sweeping statements of sustainability without supporting evidence

Table 3.2   (Continued)

	Mature sustainability leaders	Aspiring sustainability leaders	Early stages of sustainability maturity
3) Embed and develop sustainability within the organization	• Explicit ongoing sustainability training for all employees • Dedicated resources and management responsibility for sustainability • Explicit management measurement of sustainability achievements (e.g. metric in balanced scorecard) • Sustainability are core recruiting and retention messages	• Some understanding of sustainability issues, although not formally supported, developed or recognized • Individual initiatives • Fragmented efforts throughout the organization	• No formal sustainability responsibility within the organization

Source: Adapted from Babin and Nicholson (2011, p. 58).

In the following three sections, we describe the characteristics of providers across the three stages of maturity. We begin with the mature sustainability leaders stage.

Stage 3: Mature sustainability leaders

Providers in this stage are classified as reaching the level of leaders in adopting sustainability. All have achieved certification in the global sustainability standards. They create and file annual GRI reports, which are validated by third parties; they are ranked in the annual CDP evaluation and have implemented ISO 14000. One provider was evaluating the new ISO 26000 standard. All but one of these providers are signatories to the UN Global Compact. Sustainability is viewed by advisors to be an increasingly important requirement for outsourcing providers. An outsourcing specialist at KPMG spoke of the importance of global standards such as CDP and ISO in the contract and disclosure phase of outsourcing: "CDP is a key model for GITO providers to understand and to achieve CDP certification". A GITO legal advisor in London spoke of the need for sustainability standards in outsourcing contracts: "definitely out there, in the near future, as a matter of course people will expect it; [Sustainability] after some years will become boilerplate" and CDP is "unquestionably on its way". Another legal advisor in Toronto stated that "carbon credits are coming to the fore" because "they are tangible" in many jurisdictions. Regarding global sustainability standards, one CSR academic declared that "GRI opens the door to CSR, driving change psychologically" within the organization, which suggests that when organizations implement GRI they begin to change their social and environmental actions, becoming more responsible in both areas. Given this increasing importance, the mature sustainability providers have responded by participation in sustainability global standards.

Sustainability credentials help to distinguish outsourcing providers in a competitive market. In responding to requests for proposals, mature providers can demonstrate a breadth of sustainability credentials in terms of certification and external audit. As one senior outsourcing executive at Accenture told us, "carbon emission reductions will be part of many RFPs and proposals", and another executive at the same firm stated after the economic recession (2008–2009), "competition looks different in an age of sustainability development".

By proving their compliance with the major sustainability standards, the mature providers are anticipating stakeholder requirements and expectations. As one GITO regional CEO at EDS explained, the sustainability issue "train has left the station, everyone accepts this as an issue; environmental taxes and regulations will come from government, they are inevitable". This means that sustainability has become a normalized activity for mature outsourcing providers and their customers. There is no need to "sell" the sustainability concept within the mature organization. In terms of stakeholder expectations, Enbridge Gas Distribution implemented a carbon data management system to track all carbon emissions from within the company, and it has plans to include its suppliers. Another outsourcing buyer published its Environmental and Social Performance Standards for providers, which asks for documented environmental management systems and measures regarding GHG emissions and energy consumption. The implication is that more and more buyers will expect providers to comply with their increasing sustainability expectations.

Two mature GITO providers in the sample described how they offer sustainability consulting services to buyer organizations. A GITO specialist at Accenture told us of a sustainability consulting practice that had grown to 1,000 people in less than two years, offering a new and growing source of revenue for some consultancies. Another mature GITO provider, TCS, described helping a client to develop a balanced scorecard to focus on environmental issues in the outsourcing relationship. The implication is that sustainability is useful to win competitive outsourcing deals and also provides a revenue-producing line of business.

Mature GITO providers use their sustainability profile to attract and retain employees. They demonstrate and communicate their commitment to sustainability through external advertising, events and internal communication. For example, sustainability leader Accenture sent an email to all employees that boasted of a recent "strong showing" in the CDP evaluation, reflecting "robust carbon and energy measurements...implementing Environmental Management Systems across [all] operations". This same GITO provider launched an "Eco Challenge" that attracted participation from 19% of its global workforce and reduced carbon emissions by 40,000 tons. These internal statements are intended to encourage employees by acknowledging sustainability progress and to instill pride within the organization.

Stage 2: Aspiring sustainability leaders

GITO providers who aspire to sustainability maturity have begun to adopt some of the relevant global sustainability standards. However, of the seven GITO providers in this stage of maturity each one lacks participation in two or three of the sustainability global standards. Five of the firms in this category do not participate in the GRI or GRI verification. Four are not signatories to the UN Global compact. Four are not listed in any social responsibility investment (SRI) index and two do not participate in the CDP. One executive from one of the largest US GITO providers commented that sustainability is an additional tax on the outsourcing industry and should be rejected. Some GITO providers in this category may be reluctant sustainability participants, reacting to the sustainability profile established by leaders and to the growing sustainability expectations defined in buyer RFPs.

At these providers, the sustainability communication is less compelling and less complete than that evident at the sustainability leaders. The sustainability reports at aspirants do not align with standardized GRI reporting formats. For example, CSC provides financial and business operation information on its website, but it does not provide any formal sustainability report.[6] Similarly, the website of aspiring sustainability provider CGI provides examples of philanthropic contributions to charitable causes. CGI "is proud" to identify participation in the FTSE-4-Good and the Dow Jones Sustainability Index (DJSI; CGI, 2011). However, CGI does not provide an annual formal sustainability report covering all aspects of its sustainability performance. In contrast, Infosys publishes an annual sustainability report, formatted and registered according to GRI standards. Aspiring sustainability providers mainly provide sustainability reporting as part of the marketing function, which may lead to skepticism from buyers.

Several of the GITO buyers interviewed in the preliminary interviews and at Co-Operative Financial Services spoke of their personal cynicism regarding sustainability initiatives. They were concerned that stakeholders such as customers or employees would see communication as "greenwash" without substance. The interviews at CFS identified "bolt-on" CSR, which was viewed as an afterthought and was not embedded in the provider organization or the outsourcing service. They expressed caution with regard to GITO providers who crafted a marketing message but did not have a formalized, integrated CSR approach because the sustainability communication was not supported with verifiable data, such as an audited GRI report. The implication is that aspiring leaders must prove to their stakeholders that their sustainability is authentic.

Stage 1: Early stage sustainability providers

In early stage sustainability, the GITO providers in the sample have not yet adopted global sustainability standards. Of the six GITO providers in the early stages of sustainability maturity, two participate in only one global standard and four do not participate in any. Some participate in minor programs offered by other organizations. For example, GITO provider Mastek participates in the HP Planet Partner Program, which offers environment-friendly solutions for recycling printer cartridges.

Of the 19 firms analyzed in this way, the smaller firms (based on revenue) tend to be the ones who have adopted fewer or no standards. Prior research has examined the challenges that small firms face as a result of the relatively high transaction costs related to outsourcing. Small firms are disadvantaged relative to large firms in a wide range of resources crucial to coordination, which aptly describes the GITO providers in this early stage of sustainability maturity.[7]

Some early stage firms have taken actions but not yet adopted global standards. Provider ACS is replacing the roofs of its data center with green roofs, which consist of vegetation planted over a waterproofing membrane. These roofs have been demonstrated to lower the building temperature by up to 12°F. However, despite this admirable sustainability example project, ACS does not participate in the GRI and the CDP, has not signed the UN Global Compact and has not committed to implementing an ISO 14001 certified Environmental Management System.

Also characteristic of this stage, communications with stakeholders are reactive and unplanned. For instance, providers at this stage do not provide a regular sustainability report to the public. They may tend to make sweeping statements without support, such as an Indian provider's claims that it "takes care to avoid any kind of environmental pollution through its actions".

The implication is that early stage sustainability providers will be challenged by buyers and other stakeholders such as governments and NGOs to improve their sustainability profile, in order to compete with others who have greater levels of capability in the more mature stages.

Moving from early stage, to aspirant, to mature sustainability

Over four years of research, we have seen an increasing interest in the topic of sustainability in outsourcing from buyers, providers and advisors. It is difficult to imagine that some GITO providers have not yet embraced sustainability as an organizational program and market requirement. We fully expect that early stage and aspiring GITO providers will begin to report using the GRI format, moving beyond corporate sustainability brochures, and will engage in preliminary CDP evaluations. In addition, now that ISO 26000 is finalized, many aspiring firms will embrace that standard as a formalization of their early sustainability actions. It may be possible that the ISO 26000 standard will become as important to the industry as CMM and standards on quality such as ISO 9000 and security such as BS5750. This standard will require early stage and aspiring providers to establish a formal sustainability program and protocol within the organization, moving beyond a marketing and communication approach. The challenges for aspirants will be to understand when buyer sustainability requirements, as communicated in RFPs, industry guides and government regulations, exceed the cost of adopting further sustainability commitments. Corporate size and profitability will be limitations for providers who aspire to greater sustainability. Aspirants who desire to work with top GITO buyer firms (e.g. Fortune 500 or FT 100) will require a high level of sustainability accreditation (e.g. GRI, CDP) to meet their expectation. A large Indian GITO provider, for example, has upgraded its sustainability ability in order to do business with these major firms and thus sustainability capability should reflect the buyer organization sustainability norms, in order to match the "cultural fit" expectation mentioned by several of these buyers.

The discussion above has provided an overview of sustainability in the outsourcing industry by examining a set of 19 leading GITO providers. In the following sections, we build on this with a model of sustainability activity discussed in relation to two mature providers, Accenture and a large Indian GITO provider. This will offer greater detail of the sustainability practices at these mature providers and scope for comparison.

Sustainability models for business

Researchers Michael Porter and Mark Kramer[8] present a sustainability model that enables firms to better focus their efforts by integrating sustainability activity into business practices. The authors stress the interdependence of business and society and suggest that corporate social responsibility should be focused not on generic concerns but instead in the way most appropriate to each firm's strategy. They write that "Each company can identify the particular set of societal problems that it is best equipped to help resolve and from which it can gain the greatest competitive benefit."

The Porter and Kramer framework has two major components that aim to enable the selection of appropriate initiatives. The first is based on the fit of particular initiatives to the three areas of concern (see Figure 3.2).

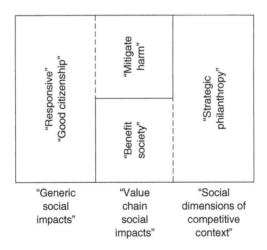

Figure 3.2 The Porter and Kramer responsive-strategic CSR framework
Source: Authors, adapted from Porter and Kramer (2006).

Each organization must select issues that intersect with its particular business, they write: "The essential test that should guide CSR is not whether a cause is worthy but whether it presents an opportunity to create shared value – that is, a meaningful benefit for society that is also valuable to the business."

The framework divides the social issues affecting an organization into three categories in order to enable choices to be made to narrow down the set of social issues that are both important and strategic for the business.

1) Generic social issues may be important to society but are neither significantly affected by the organization's operations nor influence the organization's long-term competitiveness.
2) Value chain social impacts are those that are significantly affected by the organization's activities in the ordinary course of business.
3) Social dimensions of competitive context are factors in the external environment that significantly affect the underlying drivers of competitiveness in those places where the organization operates.

Candidate social issues should be sorted into these three categories and ranked in terms of potential impact.

The second main component of the Porter and Kramer framework is establishing whether the social issue is responsive or strategic.

1) Responsive focuses on compliance, of "acting as a good corporate citizen", attuned to the evolving social concerns of stakeholders. In GITO, examples would be compliance with UN Global Compact.
2) Strategic projects are aligned initiatives where the social and business benefits are "large and distinctive". We will see examples of this in the CFS case described in Chapter 5 as well as the Accenture sustainability profile described in Chapter 4. Essentially, the outsourcing providers and buyers consciously determine how to achieve competitive advantage by focusing on social issues that are important to their own organizations and their stakeholders.

The Porter and Kramer model in Figure 3.2 advances models previously adopted by organizations (such as Archie Carroll's Pyramid from Figure 1.1 in Chapter 1), with a more focused assessment of how to consider philanthropic responsibilities. Carroll and other writers at that time recognized that business organizations are expected to provide voluntary philanthropic contributions to society, but they must first be profitable.

However, Carroll's work was a response to the views of Milton Friedman,[9] who as we discussed in Chapter 1 stated simply that "the social responsibility of business is to increase its profits". The departure for Porter and Kramer lies in the recommendation that organizations should distinguish between reactive CSR activities and CSR activities that create strategic value for the organization and for the society, the notion of *shared value*. Figure 3.3 depicts the evolution of Carroll's voluntary philanthropic model of CSR to Porter and Kramer's strategic philanthropy model.

As will be described in the next chapter, achieving the strategic benefits in an outsourcing relationship is more complicated than the models depict because of the transactional relationship between the buyer and provider and the relationship between each of them and society. Figure 3.4 depicts a model that evolves from Figure 3.3, showing the three-way relationship

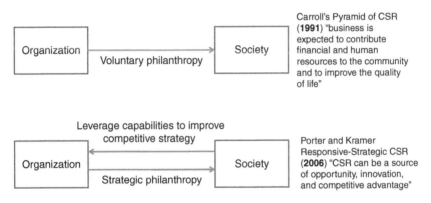

Figure 3.3 The evolving CSR model from Carroll to Porter and Kramer
Source: Authors.

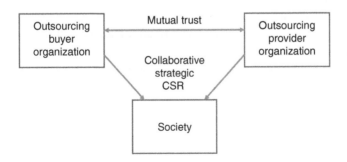

Figure 3.4 Strategic CSR in outsourcing
Source: Authors.

between provider, buyer and society. There is strategic value in outsourcing as an outcome of *collaborative sustainability*, which will be the strengthened mutual trust between the provider and buyer. Collaborative sustainability is a thoughtful and deliberate agreement, between the buyer and provider, to work together on a social or environmental issue that is important for both parties. We will explore and describe collaborative sustainability in Chapter 5.

Sustainability practices at Accenture and a large Indian outsourcing service provider

In this section, we examine sustainability at two mature outsourcing providers, Accenture and a large Indian GITO provider.

There are three key characteristics of these cases:

1) as with all large organizations these outsourcing providers protect their brand by making *philanthropic* contributions to worthy causes;
2) they demonstrate specific *strategic sustainability* practices that can be viewed through the Porter and Kramer model discussed above; and
3) at Accenture *collaborative sustainability* projects strengthen the relationship between the outsourcing buyer and provider.

In the following sections, we describe first the Accenture sustainability profile and then that of the large Indian outsourcing service provider. We describe their philanthropic sustainability, their strategic sustainability and then their collaborative sustainability.

Case 3.1: Accenture: The view from India

Accenture is a global IT service firm, which provides several categories of GITO services. For 2010, Accenture reported revenues of US$21.6 billion. According to its annual financial report, approximately 43% of Accenture revenues are from outsourcing services. Accenture employs 204,000 people around the world and is a signatory to the UN Global Compact. The Accenture 2010 annual report announced a new corporate citizenship program called "Skills to Succeed", which plans to equip 250,000 people around the world with the skills to get a job or build a business, by 2015.

Accenture's philanthropic sustainability in India

Accenture recognizes the importance of sustainability for its clients and communities and has taken steps to enhance sustainability within the organization. In India, the Accenture sustainability emphasis is on society, with less emphasis on environmental issues. Harsh Manglik, Managing Director for Accenture India, is the chairman of Accenture India and vice chair of India's software and services association NASSCOM. In 2011, Harsh became the chair of NASSCOM. His view is that client expectations are driving the importance of sustainability and its relevance in the IT outsourcing industry and that sustainability in outsourcing is a new concept, of increasing interest, in India.[10] The view that outsourcing providers are responding to buyer expectations is a message we also heard from Rio Tinto (Chapter 2). In Harsh's own words:

> people doing it (sustainability)...because it's a condition for being allowed to play the game. So long as clients are demanding sustainability any business will follow it. The implication is that providers will respond to buyer expectations, ... if buyers do not see sustainability as important, then providers would likely not bother with it.

This view may appear rather pessimistic but reflects commercial reality given that in many cases the role of outsourcing is to cut cost and GITO providers aim to satisfy their buyers. However, Accenture sustainability activity in India is focused on society and employment, which is part of a wider collective trend. In 2008, NASSCOM prepared a report regarding the impact of IT outsourcing on the Indian economy,[11] which highlights the direct and indirect economic benefits of the IT industry, as well as the contributions to workforce development and contributions to the community and the environment. According to the report, the major social contribution of the industry has been to create a motivated and educated managerial class. In addition, the industry in part through NASSCOM has taken steps to provide social contributions to individuals and communities in need of assistance. Social causes in India have tended to be prioritized over environmental issues. Accenture works with NASSCOM to target young teenage women from poor backgrounds and works with an NGO and through the NASSCOM foundation to focus on teaching computer animation skills. Under the NASSCOM foundation they intend to develop programs that leverage information and communication technologies to accelerate skill development as opposed to mainstream education. The focus here is more on the vocational aspect of skills, which in India is a huge and unmet need.

The Accenture executive for corporate citizenship in India is Kshitija Krishnaswamy who further described Accenture's sustainability focus on developing skills in the community. In her own words:

> We have a responsibility to the communities that we operate out of; our people have responsibilities towards that individually and as an organization collectively. We would like to make a social difference, to make some sort of social impact. We have a mandate which is "Building Skills to Succeed". As an organization we would like to ensure that young people can contribute to the economy. We look at vocational skilling; India's need is in the area of livelihood generation.

The implication here is that philanthropic sustainability is an important trend for the Indian GITO industry, but the emphasis tends toward social issues such as developing skills for employment. This contrasts with the relative importance given to environmental issues by North American GITO firms (see Chapter 2).

Accenture's strategic sustainability

Accenture uses sustainability activities strategically to build a potential future pool of employees. Corporate citizenship executive Kshitija Krishnaswamy stated that Accenture is focusing on developing skills for its outsourcing business so that it will have a pool of talent for future employment. "We've actually identified industries that have the highest potential for employment; we are in the service industry so we have started with IT and business process outsourcing skills." The value is shared: Accenture benefits with potential future employees, the young trainees benefit from a set of market-relevant skills and Accenture employees benefit from the sense of satisfaction as a result of the contributions they make to their community.

Accenture's collaborative sustainability

Strategic use of sustainability can build a stronger relationship between the buyer and provider. Accenture management told us about the firm's collaborative relationship with its client, Royal Sun Alliance (RSA), which was initiated by employees at RSA.

Senior RSA executives initiated discussions between the Accenture and RSA CSR managers to explore collaboration on sustainability projects. RSA holds regular charity days that involved only UK-based staff. Two thousand Accenture staff work on the RSA account, mostly in India. The two CSR managers agreed that although the workers were Accenture employees, because they were so involved in RSA's operations day to day, eventually they needed to more closely align themselves with RSA's goals. Collaboration on the charity day was a good opportunity. The day they had charity day in London, Accenture India structured an RSA-funded charity day for those 2,000 employees in India. The results were positive, in the words of the Accenture manager: "it helped RSA get closer to the Accenture people who have been on their account ever since we got the business. And it's something they're having annually now."

This is another example of shared value because the buyer, provider and society all share in the value from the collaboration. The buyer gets closer to the provider staff, who works on their account; a charity receives a larger monetary contribution from the buyer that has been augmented with donations from the provider; the provider gets a deeper relationship with the buyer.

Summary of Accenture's sustainability

Sustainability issues at Accenture continue to increase in importance. For example, working with the World Business Council for Sustainable Development in 2009, Accenture published an assessment of the impact of sustainability on corporate strategies.[12] In 2010, Accenture worked with the United Nations to publish a report on the new era of sustainability.[13] Accenture now recognizes sustainability as a topic that has grown well beyond the basic economic value of Green IT initially described in 2007.[14] The implication of this is clear: as a leading GITO provider, Accenture has recognized the importance of sustainability for clients, employees, society and the environment and has taken steps to increase its sustainability credentials. Accenture applied sustainability principles both to address social issues such as skill development in regions where desired skills are low but the employee pool is compelling, and collaboratively to strengthen outsourcing relationships with GITO buyers. In the next section, we will examine a large Indian outsourcing provider that has taken similar steps.

Case 3.2: Sustainability at the Indian GITO provider

The Indian GITO provider is also a mature sustainability leader. This case describes the emphasis that the Indian GITO provider puts on environmental responsibility. It is one of the largest GITO providers in India, with 114,000 employees providing service to 575 clients in 72 cities across 30 different countries. In 2010, the large Indian outsourcing provider reported annual revenues of US$1.3 billion. It is a signatory to the UN Global Compact and prepares an annual sustainability report that is formatted according to the GRI framework and is audited by an independent assurance organization. According to the sustainability report,

> our focus on social and environmental issues is fundamental to our existence in the long term. We intend to take a more holistic view of our sustainability by setting up a framework and governance structure.... We will strive to become... a carbon neutral, water sustainable and socially meaningful business.

The Indian outsourcing service provider adopted a sustainability policy in July 2010, which begins with the foundational premise that the business must be profitable to be sustainable, stating that the Indian GITO provider will follow a "model of profitability, sustainability, predictability and de-risking our business while ensuring a green planet". Moreover, the Indian outsourcing service provider acknowledges that it must work with clients to make their businesses profitable and sustainable, stating "We want to enhance business value leverage to our clients from transactions with us, while ensuring sustainability for them by helping them achieve their sustainability goals". The voluntary sustainability component of the Indian GITO provider sustainability policy contains three parts.

1) First, the Indian GITO provider will be resource efficient with short-term goals of reducing per capita consumption of electricity, water and carbon emissions, and a long-term goal of becoming water sustainable and carbon neutral.
2) Second, it will embrace green innovation by investing in green building and data centers to effectively utilize natural resources and to encourage vendors to become more focused on their green initiatives.
3) Third, it acknowledges the social contract it has with customers, employees, investors, communities and the global population, and actively engages these stakeholders.

The Indian outsourcing service provider began reporting on sustainability in 2008 and claimed that it was the first Indian outsourcing provider to do so. Consistent with survey data depicted in Figure 4.1, the Indian GITO provider sustainability leader commented that:

> today sustainability is in the RFP, they (clients) ask how conscious you are about sustainability, what are your policies... It's part of the RFP process but I don't know if it's really the deciding criterion yet.... I think it will become a very big criterion at some point.

India GITO provider philanthropic sustainability

The philanthropic sustainability for the Indian GITO provider covers five topics using the acronym HEART: Health care; Education; Art and culture; Rural uplift and rehabilitation and Targeted inclusive growth.

These sustainability topics are supported by financial contributions from the Foundation and the Science Foundation. Each year, the Corporation makes voluntary financial contributions to these two foundations, which then direct the funds to specific projects in the Indian community. For example, the Foundation has provided books to more than 3,000 schools in India and has provided scholarships to 4,500 poor students.

India GITO provider strategic sustainability

The sustainability practice emphasizes environmental responsibility, which has been identified as one of the CEO's top seven priorities. There are three areas of focus within that initiative:

1) power consumption in data centers and office facilities;
2) individual carbon footprint; and
3) water consumption.

Power consumption

The Indian GITO provider is developing innovative techniques to reduce power consumption, thus reducing its overall carbon footprint. The head of the green initiatives stated:

> In a data center, the biggest issue is how much energy is being consumed. At an average data center for every one unit of electricity consumed by computers and servers, there is one unit of electricity consumed for miscellaneous such as air-conditioning, lighting and other purposes.

To improve the power utilization efficiency of its data centers, the Indian outsourcing service provider has been conducting research and development on use of sensors in data centers for on-demand cooling. Heat flows in the rack can continuously change depending on how much the servers are being stressed. Radiant cooling panels behind server racks provide on-demand cooling to the rack that it requires. In addition, the Indian outsourcing service provider has implemented sensors in its office locations that switch lights and other power consumption off when human activity is not detected. Finally, with regard to power consumption, the Indian GITO provider is investing in research on efficient cooling technology, because buildings consume 40% of all the energy and therefore are responsible for 40% of all the carbon emissions. Of that consumption, 50% is attributable to air-conditioning. Management of power consumption is viewed as an opportunity to help clients and gain new consulting revenue streams.

Individual carbon footprint

The large Indian GITO provider tracks the ecological impact of employees through a personal information page on the intranet. We saw a brief demonstration of the software that tracks and creates an awareness of GHG emissions primarily caused by individual travel and commuting as well as paper consumption. Using this software, the Indian GITO provider is able to track per capita GHG emissions, by category, and take action to reduce annual consumption. In 2010, they reported year-over-year reductions in GHG for two of the three major emission categories.

Water conservation

The Indian outsourcing service provider continues to expand its employee workforce, hiring about 20,000 new employees each year. At their campus near Bangalore, which accommodates about 10,000 employees, the Indian outsourcing service provider is focused on water conservation. According to the head of the green initiatives:

> Water is something which we are very paranoid about. We feel that it's a bigger problem than climate change; it's a problem that is going to affect most of us very quickly because of unsustainable use. There are no alternatives to water. We are striving to become water neutral. At every campus that we design, it will be designed based on water conservation, which means we will survive only on rainwater for all the fresh water needs and on recycled water for all other needs.

The combined investment in power consumption management, water conservation and managing individual carbon impact characterizes the large Indian outsourcing provider as a sustainability GITO leader. However, we found no evidence that the Indian outsourcing provider has begun to use sustainability in collaboration with clients, as we discuss in the next section.

Comparison of Accenture and the large Indian GITO provider sustainability

Both Accenture and the Indian outsourcing service provider are leading GITO providers and mature sustainability leaders, but they embrace sustainability in different ways and will achieve different benefits. Both firms are signatories to the UN Global Compact and both firms have worked with the World Business Council for Sustainable Development to develop a vision of sustainability for the next 40 years.[15] The large Indian GITO provider has focused on sustainability needs in India and on the environment in the large campuses where water conservation, for example, is critical to operations. The Indian GITO provider publishes an annual sustainability report, using GRI protocol, as evidence of its social and environmental responsibility. Accenture publishes customer- and market-oriented "thought leadership" reports that are intended to inform clients and sell Accenture services. Accenture has not yet published an organization-wide GRI sustainability report. Accenture has begun to embrace collaborative sustainability, whereas the large Indian GITO provider has not yet shown evidence of this approach.

Introducing the sustainable global outsourcing model

The findings point to multiple roles and rationales for sustainability in outsourcing, which we have divided into two categories: responsive and strategic. The responsive category has two elements:

1) acting as a good corporate citizen, attuned to the evolving social expectations and needs of stakeholders; and
2) mitigating existing or adverse effects from business activities.

The strategic category involves initiatives where social and business benefits are distinctive and provide long-term competitive advantage, and create shared value for society. Our model adds the concept of collaborative sustainability where outsourcing buyers and providers work together on joint sustainability projects. Figure 3.5 is an illustration of a model for a sustainability hierarchy for GITO.

In the sections below, we describe examples for each level of the sustainability hierarchy depicted in Figure 3.5, beginning with collaborative sustainability. The examples will be drawn from the pilot case studies

Figure 3.5   Sustainable GITO model
Source: Authors.

described in Chapter 2, at Enbridge and Rio Tinto, and from review of providers Accenture and the Indian GITO provider described above.

Collaborative sustainability in global IT outsourcing

Collaborative sustainability provides the highest level of shared value for outsourcing buyers and providers, yet very few are participating in this sustainability level. Accenture provides one example of collaborative sustainability, with an intention to gain benefit from the sustainability activity. Kshitija Krishnaswamy commented that Accenture was contemplating how to apply the success of the shared charity day conducted with RSA in other ways:

> We've done this [sustainability] activity just for ourselves; we started thinking about how to get clients involved...We start informally; our senior executives have started telling them about it...We are trying to structure value propositions that we take to clients saying "this makes sense"...to deepen our own client relationship or start a new one.

Accenture anticipates that working with buyers on sustainability projects will strengthen the relationship. In Chapter 4, we examine collaborative sustainability in greater depth.

Strategic sustainability in global IT outsourcing

Strategic sustainability is about choosing a unique position, doing things differently from competitors in a way that lowers costs or better serves a particular set of customer needs. It unlocks shared value by investing in social aspects of context that strengthen company competitiveness.[16] In our research, we identified two strategic practices by which sustainability strengthens outsourcing competitiveness:

1) Sustainability improves the outsourcing relationship by building trust between buyer and provider.
2) New and growing revenue opportunities are available to providers who deliver sustainability leadership and services to buyers.

These points are elaborated further below with examples of strategic sustainability from the cases we have already reviewed.

Sustainability activities improve trust

The alignment of social and environmental commitments between outsourcing buyer and provider creates and reinforces trust in a business relationship.[17] This trust extends well beyond the contractual commitments and RFP evaluations. Referring to a recent outsourcing RFP, a buyer at Rio Tinto in Montreal told us that "cultural fit, that is the values that we share, is becoming very important, especially when price difference [between providers] is marginal". The need for trust is magnified in global outsourcing because of the added complications of differences in time zone, legal system, language and culture, which make complete contracting very difficult with a greater risk of unforeseen problems. The development of sustainability measures does not preclude the parties from building trust in other ways, such as reliable delivery of services, shared risk and reward, clear communication channels, etc., but it does provide a convenient and tangible mechanism for bringing the two parties closer together, through developing shared values.

Providers will deliver new sustainable value-added services

Leading outsourcing providers are building a growing line of business in providing sustainability consulting services to outsourcing buyers. The new offerings may come from providers who have developed expertise from their internal sustainability projects or may be delivered by newly acquired sustainability experts.

Case 3.3: Enbridge responds to the tsunami disaster

North American outsourcing buyer Enbridge described its relationship with Accenture's operations in south-east Asia. When the 2004 tsunami hit that region, the Enbridge office staff in Toronto responded with a fund-raising initiative to help their colleagues in the provider firm. Although the offices were on opposite sides of the world, the "faceless" relationship had become tangible, and the effort helped strengthen the relationship and trust between the individuals in the two organizations.

The large Indian outsourcing service provider and Accenture told us how they offer sustainability consulting services to buyers. One outsourcing executive at Accenture told us of their sustainability consulting practice that had grown to employ 1,000 people in less than two years. The Indian GITO provider has demonstrated an ability to reduce power consumption in IT operations, thereby reducing GHG emissions and lowering operating costs.

In summary, developing strategic sustainability practices is an opportunity for outsourcing providers to gain competitive advantage in two ways – by enhancing the relationship with their buyers and by delivering new sustainability consulting services.

Responsive sustainability in global IT outsourcing

Many sustainability actions in outsourcing appear to be reactive, prompted perhaps by a client sustainability requirement in an RFP or compliance with a government regulation such as the UK Carbon Reduction Commitment. These actions are responsive, where outsourcing providers act as good corporate citizens. Below we describe how providers react to the evolving social and environmental concerns of buyers, government regulators, employees and others.

Outsourcing providers must exceed buyer sustainability expectations

We initially expected that buyer requirements would drive outsourcing provider sustainability capabilities. This was confirmed with evidence from buyers such as Rio Tinto's RFP requirement, which stated the importance of cultural fit and shared sustainability values when evaluating an outsourcing provider. Buyers expect outsourcing providers to bring a sustainability capability that will not diminish the buyer's reputation.

As one buyer at Enbridge explained, "Our own environmental responsibility builds our brand and trust. This reputation brings and retains our customers." "When we look at the outsourcer's [sustainability profile] we must balance cost [benefits] with the impact to our brand." In other words, the buyer seeks lower operating costs through outsourcing, but not if outsourcing threatens its sustainability reputation.

Outsourcing providers comply with sustainability regulations

Chapter 1 demonstrated how domestic policy makers and world leaders are concerned about the emission of GHGs that contribute to global warming. The production of electricity often requires the burning of fossil fuels, such as natural gas or coal, which produces GHGs. In the last decade, the general public has become aware and concerned about global warming and the resultant climate changes. Governments in many countries are now adopting laws and regulations to curb or diminish the consumption of electrical power and the burning of fossil fuels. For example, in 2009 the UK government implemented the Carbon Reduction Commitment requiring an estimated 5,000 UK organizations to reduce electrical power consumption through a set of incentives and penalties. The Australian government introduced a carbon tax in 2011. In 2008, the European Union published a Code of Conduct for Data Centres Efficiency. These laws and regulations have an impact on outsourcing providers, especially those who specialize in outsourcing of data centers, which are high electrical power consumers. A Toronto-based EDS executive stated that in British Columbia, data centers are now required to comply with government goals to reduce GHGs by 30% by 2020. His view was that this would be difficult to achieve with outsourced data centers that were built "when power was cheap". As a result, as we saw at the Indian outsourcing service provider, GITO providers will need to develop innovative solutions to reduce data center power consumption to meet these regulations.

Outsourcing providers must respond to employee sustainability expectations and needs

A recent sustainability initiative survey from MIT researchers demonstrates that sustainability has an impact on employee recruitment and retention. The survey found that "of private companies 57% say they expect employee interest in sustainability to impact their organizations" and "37% [had] already highlighted sustainability initiatives in recruiting".[18] At CFS in the United Kingdom, the CIO stressed the importance of sustainability in retaining employees and nurturing new ones. At Rio Tinto in Montreal, the director of sustainable development described the importance of employee and family health. In areas where malaria is prevalent, worker absenteeism can be problematic when workers care for their sick family member or are themselves ill. Rio Tinto invests in measures to prevent malaria, which are a reasonable sustainability action to improve worker attendance.

At Accenture India, Kshitija Krishnaswamy, the head of corporate citizenship, commented on employee motivation from sustainability. In her own words: "Our people then volunteer to take guest lectures. Our people mentor the students. We get probably better impact because our people are engaged with the agenda of an organization. They feel they are part of something bigger than their own jobs." These comments agree with findings from the Co-operative case study, which we will present in Chapter 4.

Providers will use sustainability to defend the corporate brand

Sustainability initiatives can be seen as brand insurance by outsourcing buyers and providers.[19] In an example, which will be discussed in more detail in Chapter 4, CFS has gone so far as to seek outsourcers with strong sustainability reputations to re-enforce the value of its own corporate brand. The buyer sees sustainability as the "missing link" in global outsourcing and the opportunity for "leveraging [sustainability] toward brand equity" for both the buyer and the provider, as described by the head of IT Outsourcing at CFS. This UK firm has turned away loan applications from potential clients and dismissed outsourcing providers who did not measure up to the firm's own sustainability levels.

As another example, Enbridge described how sustainability and its impact on corporate brand would soon be included as a metric in its corporate and personal balanced scorecard. Not surprisingly, outsourcing provider TCS is committed to embrace environmental issues with Enbridge. The provider will develop sustainability initiatives with the client that can be measured in a meaningful way so that they can be included in a balanced scorecard. TCS is using environmental aspects of sustainability to build its brand with the Enbridge buyers.

Outsourcing providers will reduce costs with green outsourcing

Environmental responsibility in outsourcing is driven largely by increasing power costs. However, the threat of negative publicity and regulation on reduced carbon emissions suggests that Green Outsourcing will be a growing requirement. Most outsourcing providers are major consumers of electrical power. Several commentators predict a long-term trend of rising energy demand and costs.[20] As well, power consumption by IT doubled from 2000 to 2005 according to the US Environmental Protection Agency[21] and continues to grow, albeit at a slower rate.[22] Rising costs of electrical power and increased power demand in IT creates a concern regarding the rising costs in outsourced IT operations. The 2009 Green Outsourcing Survey reported that 85% of the senior executives surveyed said that "the adoption of green technology is more likely the result of escalating energy costs than ecological altruism".[23]

Reacting to this trend, the large Indian GITO provider has established reduction of power consumption in the data center as an important sustainability goal. In our visit to their offices in India we learned how their sustainability team is developing innovative approaches to provide low-cost on-demand cooling and lighting for the data center. Lower power costs are important in addition to the lower carbon emissions. Both issues are a priority for the Indian GITO provider, because, as described by the head of green initiatives, buyers are "embedding sustainability into the business processes" and expect their providers to help them reduce their carbon footprint and power costs.

Outsourcing provides a path for buyers to reduce escalating technology costs and the associated GHG emissions from increased power consumption. Saving money through "green" outsourcing is a strong reactive sustainability motivation for many buyers.

Philanthropic sustainability in global IT outsourcing

The Indian outsource provider makes annual voluntary financial contributions to two philanthropic foundations, which administer the funds separately from the GITO operations. The contributions can only be made if Indian outsource operations are profitable. Similarly, Accenture makes voluntary contributions of resources, often paid effort by its consultants, to charitable causes, such as the contribution to improve employable skills in India. One charitable recipient of Accenture philanthropy is Nethope, which is a global shared service that supports humanitarian and disaster relief activities through delivery of ICT services.[24] Accenture is the primary GITO supporter to Nethope, contributing consulting effort and funds.

Table 3.3 summarizes our collaborative, strategic, responsive and philanthropic sustainability examples in GITO.

Table 3.3   Examples in the sustainable GITO model

Hierarchy of sustainability in GITO	Example	Outsourcing *buyer*/provider
Collaborative	Collaborate with clients on shared charity day	*RSA*/Accenture
	Collaborate on sustainability education projects (Chapter 4)	*CFS*/Steria
Strategic	Improve the outsourcing relationship	*Rio Tinto*
	• Cultural fit and shared values	*Enbridge*/ Accenture
	• Helping out after tsunami disaster	
	• Sustainability consulting services	Accenture
	• Energy efficient data centers	
Responsive	Outsourcing providers must exceed buyer sustainability expectations	*Rio Tinto*
	Outsourcing providers comply with sustainability regulations	*BC Government*/EDS
	Must respond to employee sustainability expectations and needs	*Rio Tinto*
		Accenture
	Sustainability defends the corporate brand	*CFS*
		Enbridge/TCS
	Outsourcing providers reduce costs with Green Outsourcing	
Philanthropic	Contributions of time and effort to charitable causes	Foundation
		Building Skills to Succeed/Accenture
		Nethope/Accenture

Source: Authors.

Conclusion

The purpose of this chapter is to develop our understanding of sustainability in GITO providers. By examining public sustainability information of leading GITO providers, we are able to define three levels of sustainability maturity. Examining adoption of global sustainability standards, ability to communicate with stakeholders and how sustainability capabilities are embedded within an organization enables GITO providers to measure and improve their sustainability performance. Similarly, buyers can compare and evaluate the sustainability maturity of their providers for provider selection or to encourage aspiring or early stage GITO providers to develop their sustainability. The specific examples of sustainability at

Accenture and a large Indian GITO provider, both mature sustainability leaders, demonstrate the practices that these leading firms have adopted. The next chapter will further develop the concept of collaborative sustainability in a case study of the relationship between outsourcing buyer CFS and outsourcing provider Steria.

4
Collaborating for Shared Value

NGOs, governments, and companies must stop thinking in terms of "corporate social responsibility" and start thinking in terms of "corporate social integration".

Michael Porter[1]

How you treat your staff and the environment you operate in is really, really key to us in a longer-term outsourcing relationship.

Jim Slack, CIO, Co-operative Financial Services

Introduction

The accumulated evidence is clear: the importance of sustainability is growing for all organizations. Employees, customers, shareholders, governments, unions and NGOs increasingly expect both public and private organizations to behave responsibly toward individuals, to society and to the planet on which we live. At the same time, as we demonstrated in Chapter 1, global outsourcing of IT has become an important and accepted approach by which organizations can reduce costs and remain competitive. Chapter 2 showed how outsourcing buyers and providers integrate sustainability into relationships, from RFP onward. Chapter 3 focused on identifying the sustainability maturity of providers and introduced some practices for collaboration on sustainability projects that bring benefits. In this chapter, we focus in detail on the competitive advantages that may be accrued from collaboration and the practices that enable such benefits. Here, we focus on the role of sustainability in the management of established relationships, as opposed to early stage supplier selection activity. The benefits that may be accrued from collaboration on sustainability projects are illustrated with the case study of the UK-based CFS and its outsourcing provider Steria. Managed effectively, collaboration on shared sustainability projects strengthens the outsourcing relationship by building trust in various ways between buyer and provider employees. This chapter proceeds by firstly describing the relationship between CFS and Steria and the sustainability project on which they collaborate. Following this, the six key management lessons from the case are discussed. These lessons are carried into Chapter 5 where we present a toolset for collaborative sustainability management action.

Collaboration and trust

Collaboration is a co-operative arrangement in which two or more parties work jointly in common enterprise toward a shared goal. This implies close partnering, developed over and for the long term, distinguished by reciprocity risk sharing, investment of resources and time.[2] Trust plays a very important part in collaboration in outsourcing relationships. Figure 4.1 shows the parallel development of contractual and relationship governance between the buyer and the provider. A smooth outsourcing working relationship is largely a task of monitoring the key performance indicators (KPIs) in the contract as well as the communication and cooperation between the parties, both of which are linked to the development of trust. Social and personal bonds between individuals are important to the

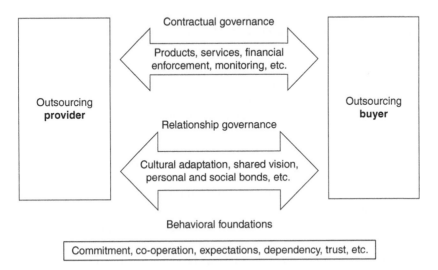

Figure 4.1 Outsourcing relationship governance framework and the role of trust
Source: Adapted from Kern and Willcocks (2000).

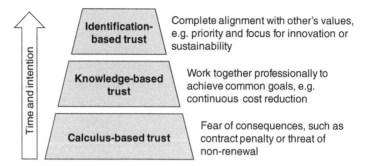

Figure 4.2 Hierarchy of trust
Source: Lewicki and Bunker (1996).

relationship, as are shared cultural beliefs and values. Relationship governance is not required for all outsourcing relationships. Commodity processing of programmable repeatable activity can be accomplished with the application of arm's-length contracts and associated KPIs. However, more sophisticated mission-critical services such as large-scale IT development requires a trust-based relationship.

Contractual governance is based on calculus-based trust,[3] ensuring consistency of behavior by imposing penalties for non-conformance. An example would be contractual clauses related to financial consequences imposed on a provider for not meeting a KPI. Relationship governance is concerned with knowledge-based trust and is based on track record of success. Knowledge-based trust occurs when a buyer (or provider) has enough information over time (Service Level Agreement's met, problems solved, etc.) to accurately anticipate likely behavior. Identification-based trust is based on empathy with the other party's desires and intentions. At this third level, trust exists because each party mutually understands, agrees with and empathizes with the values of the other (Figure 4.2).

Sustainability collaboration and shared value

How are sustainability projects and improvements in trust related? In Chapter 3, we discussed the notion of responsive and strategic sustainability based on the research from Harvard University, USA. In this chapter, we add another category: collaborative sustainability.

Figure 4.3 depicts the concept of collaborative sustainability, which sits above the strategic actions described by Porter and Kramer. Outsourcing

Figure 4.3 Hierarchy of sustainability in outsourcing
Source: Authors.

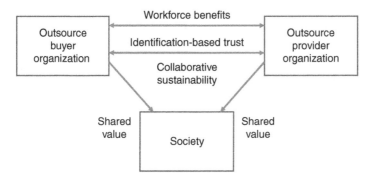

Figure 4.4 Shared sustainability value
Source: Authors.

provides a unique opportunity for strategic sustainability because of the relationship between the buyer and the provider.

Strategic and collaborative providers define their sustainability projects and work with buyers to build knowledge and identification-based trust in the relationship. The result of this is a win-win scenario for the good causes that are sponsored of a social or environmental nature, and the result of improved trust relations between the outsourcing partners shown in Figure 4.4. Let us now bring these ideas to life with a case study.

Case 4.1: Sustainability collaboration: Learning from CFS and Steria

CFS is part of The Co-operative Group, the United Kingdom's largest consumer co-operative. CFS is a group of businesses that includes The Co-operative Insurance and The Co-operative Bank, incorporating Internet bank Smile and Britannia Building Society. CFS revenues for 2010 were £550 million. The Co-operative has 12,000 employees in more than 300 branches and 20 corporate banking centers. Ethical, environmental and community matters take a high priority at CFS, and there are a range of ethical policies setting out the way the firm conducts business, most of which have been developed in consultation with customers, many of whom are also members. The Co-operative's social responsibility focus has deep foundations, which date back to 1844 when it began as the Rochdale Society of Equitable Pioneers, whose goal was the "improvement of the social and domestic condition of its members".[4] The Co-operative Group's annual report[5] states that:

> our members are our owners ... we run our business for the benefit of our members who share in our profits in proportion to how much they trade with us throughout the year. That means that our members are involved in democratic decision-making. Our members also set our social and campaigning agenda. In fact, because our members wanted it, we've become pioneers in areas such as fair-trade and combating climate change.

The local social objectives of the Rochdale Pioneers have evolved to become the Co-operative Group's focus on global sustainability, and today the Co-operative balances profitable operations with a "purpose beyond profit" and with a goal to "show the way forward for corporate sustainable development in the United Kingdom". The Co-op Values and Principles Committee is responsible for establishing social and environmental priorities and for managing the firm's ethical operating plan. The ethical operating plan establishes social and environmental goals in the areas of ethical finance, tackling global poverty, protecting the environment, inspiring young people and keeping communities thriving. Progress is reported annually in a sustainability report. The Co-operative has been recognized for its sustainable leadership with an Environmental Leadership Award in 2009 from Business in the Community and for its corporate responsibility (CR) with a Platinum Plus ranking in 2010.

CFS believes that sustainability distinguishes it from competitors, and that this advantage is challenged by others in the marketplace, such as HSBC. CFS continues to reinforce its advantage in this area. As one CFS executive explained: "People see us as leading but other organizations are catching up quickly... everybody is on the bandwagon. We need to up our game and up the stakes. We've got to keep pushing the boundaries to maintain our reputation." Maintaining the leadership position of CFS in sustainability is a significant motivating factor for collaborating with GITO providers.

Steria

The outsourcing relationship between CFS and Steria (previously Xansa) began in the 1990s. Steria's work is primarily focused on the maintenance and support of legacy software applications at CFS. In 2009, the total expenditure of CFS with Steria represented more than 20% of the overall outsourcing spend.

Compared to global IT service companies such as IBM, Accenture and others, Steria is a mid-tier, regional firm and ranks itself as Europe's ninth largest IT service provider with 1.2% of the market share in Western Europe. Steria employs more than 18,600 employees across 16 countries and has offices in Europe, India, North Africa and South East Asia. Headquartered in Paris, revenues in 2010 were €1.7 billion. Steria's main business is consulting and systems integration (51% of revenue) and IT infrastructure management (31% of revenue), with additional revenues from BPO and third-party applications maintenance. Steria speaks proudly of its social responsibility reputation. For example, according to the Steria corporate registration document, the governance model has included employee shareholders since its foundation in 1969, and currently 20% of the capital of Steria is held by employees. Steria is a member of the UN Global Compact. In 2008 and 2009, Steria was recognized for its sustainability activities in India, receiving the best practice award sponsored by the NASSCOM Foundation and the Bombay Stock Exchange. Steria's focus on CSR has a dual focus on the environment, "proactively participating in the support of a sustainable world for all" and on social responsibility, "bringing greater independence to disadvantaged people". In its corporate strategy Steria identifies the need to "reconcile development and social responsibility". Steria is "dedicated to the fight against digital divide and exclusion [with] its support for the most disadvantaged in India".[6] Steria has focused on education in India for underprivileged children and those in rural communities with an emphasis on young women. This aligns with two of the social responsibility priorities of CFS: "international development" and "inspiring young people" and is an example of the cultural fit between Steria and CFS.

The Steria–CFS sustainability partnership project

The Steria sustainability strategy has four categories relating to priorities in environment, marketplace, workplace and community, which include access to IT and education. In the latter category the "One Steria One Country One School" (OSOCOS) program is offered to selected buyers as a route to partnering by injecting resource into schools located in the Indian cities of Chennai, Pune or Noida, where Steria centers are located (see Figure 4.5). The program is structured as a three-year commitment for the buyers. Steria and their buyers supported 15 schools as of May 2010. According to Steria's corporate presentation to buyers, the arrangement enables the buyer to involve staff, family and friends in the India project, to publicize the project when visiting India and to list involvement in marketing material. The buyer is presented with a "menu" of engagement options and a price list (see Table 4.1). Steria encourages partnering buyers to communicate with the children in the school through "mentorship" that may involve email, video conferencing and scheduled visits. When visiting Steria centers, buyer staff (usually high-ranking executives) are encouraged to visit the school they have sponsored. Steria refers to this arrangement as a "community collaboration procedure". Steria employees provide volunteer training and support for the schools.

	Chennai – 23 projects	Noida – 20 projects	Pune – 17 projects
Schools	15	10	11
Orphanages	4	3	1
Hospitals	1		
In-house programs	3	3	3
Other		4 rural and slum projects, adult literacy	2 schools for special children

Awards: CSR Best Practice Award, Bombay Stock Exchange, 2009, 2010.
Social Innovation Award, NASSCOM Foundation, 2010.
Special Commendations for CSR – Golden Peacock Award, 2010.

Figure 4.5   Steria sustainability projects in India

Table 4.1 Elements of Steria–CFS sustainability project at Medavakkam
High School

Computer center with ten computers
Painting, woodwork, furniture and minor civil works for computer center
 and library
Library books, language software and educational CDs and internet
 connectivity
Sports equipment and coaching sessions for one year
Environment awareness campaigns – four per year
Theatre workshops – including costumes and stage props – four per year
Mentorship sessions, sports day, study trips, other workshops and
 learning sessions

Source: Steria.

As an example, at the Medavakkam high school in Chennai, the Steria volunteers provided the following support:

- a training program, delivered at the Steria offices, to teach computer basics to the teachers, covering Microsoft Word, Excel, PowerPoint and the Internet usage;
- computer helpdesk support at the school with weekly visits to answer queries;
- a mentorship program to grade nine students, with one-hour visits each week to help the children to improve their English language skills; and
- a motivational workshop on career awareness skills and the importance of goal setting.

Steria has implemented the OSOCOS program in conjunction with eight different outsourcing buyers, including CFS. In addition to buyers, other Steria regions such as Norway and Denmark also support the OSOCOS program. Steria claims that 47,000 students have been given access to education through this program.

The process for identifying school projects is coordinated by a Steria vice president who is responsible for sustainability in India. The projects are identified by Steria members in the community, by heads of schools and by local authorities. Identified projects are assessed by Steria for appropriateness. For example, proposals are reviewed to determine whether the children are in need of additional support, the project is legitimate and the support would be well used. The school projects are then offered to buyers and to other Steria office locations for consideration. A buyer may support a full project or a portion of a project. For example, a buyer may choose to support only the computer center at a school, whereas another buyer may support the library at the same school.

Of the 15 schools supported by Steria, two have been sponsored by CFS; the first of these is Medavakkam high school, which has been sponsored since 2007. CFS has supported a computer center with ten new computers and a library. The Steria involvement there is ongoing, for instance in July 2007 Steria volunteers provided 12 days of computer training.

The second school sponsored by CFS is the Shri Ghanshyam Sharma Memorial High School in Dujana, Noida. It was established in 1999 and has 1,035 students aged 5–15 years. Children are from families sustained by low-income jobs such as farming. CFS sponsorship commenced in May 2010 with a budget of £15,714 covering the activities listed in Figure 4.5. The CFS contribution covers the initial equipment purchase, and Steria volunteers provide ongoing support such as software upgrades and technical support. CFS is not obliged to provide continuing support beyond the initial contribution, although it is encouraged to continue the relationship and to consider new OSOCOS projects.

The involvement of CFS goes beyond the simple philanthropic writing of cheques to a good charitable cause. Senior executives from both CFS and Steria participate together in annual visits to the sponsored schools. Students and school staff welcome the CFS executives and provide updates to CFS executives on their success and progress. For example, Steria provides CFS with board exam results for the classes at sponsored schools. Other Steria buyers have allowed their employees to participate in the OSOCOS Program. In 2008, employees from Lloyds TSB in London visited their sponsored school in Pune to participate in community activities. When they returned to London, the group of employees raised additional funds to contribute to the school.

CFS' commitment to the OSOCOS program is actively supported at the highest executive level. Tim Franklin, chief operating officer at CFS, is the overall project sponsor and is quoted in the Steria CR summary as saying: "Steria's school program is leaving an indelible legacy in the communities in which they serve – and CFS is hugely proud to be involved." The CFS Chief Information Officer (CIO), Jim Slack, commented on how pleased he was with the warm appreciation from students when he visited the Medavakkam high school and his desire to continue supporting the schools in India. Similarly Steve Briggs, CFS Head of Strategic Outsourcing Partnerships, commented on how the Steria outsourcing relationship was strengthened after his visit to the Medavakkam high school.

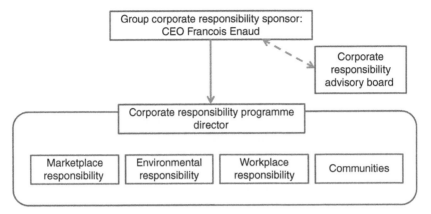

Figure 4.6 Steria – Corporate responsibility organization
Source: Steria management interviews

Steria's sustainability governance model is illustrated in Figure 4.6. Steria's CR structure is led by CEO Francois Enaud; the CEO's personal leadership of CR matters indicates the importance of CR for Steria. A director is responsible for the overall CR program, which has four components: marketplace responsibility, environmental responsibility, workplace responsibility and communities. The OSOCOS program falls within the communities component. Each component has an executive committee sponsor and one or more network leaders located in different global regions. In India, the community's network leader, who coordinates the OSOCOS program, is Vice President Gayathri Mohan.

OSOCOS provides a strong foundation for shared values between the outsourcing buyer and provider. The focus of the sustainability activity, aiding underprivileged students, is a priority for both organizations. Both parties benefit from joint visits and monitoring of the students' progress. The benefit comes from combined efforts to address a societal problem that both Steria and CFS agree is a priority. By working together and by actively participating in the program, the buyer and provider build trust, which has been described by several researchers as beneficial to the outsourcing relationship.[7]

Porter and Kramer describe strategic sustainability as moving "beyond good corporate citizenship and mitigating harmful value chain impacts to mount a small number of initiatives whose social and business benefits are large and distinctive".[8] The Co-operative Group identified "three clear priorities for community investment" in its 2009 sustainability report, which are:

- inspiring young people, where the Co-operative commits to nurturing and supporting young people;
- tackling global poverty, where the Co-operative will help support people in the developing world; and
- combating climate change.

OSOCOS links to the first two Co-operative priorities. Education for needy children in India is also important for Steria because of the growing need for skilled and dedicated workers in the Indian outsourcing centers. Interestingly, Steria is beginning to invest in solar-powered computer centers at the schools, which is a project that will align with the climate change sustainability priority of CFS.

When we look at the project from the provider perspective, Steria has created "a unique value proposition: a set of needs that a company can meet for its chosen customers that others cannot. The most strategic [sustainability] occurs when a company adds a social dimension to its value proposition making social impact integral to the overall strategy."[9]

Steria provides a commodity service – outsourcing of software application support – where competition is based heavily on price. The commodity service, such as support for standard software (e.g. Microsoft Windows), can be delivered by many outsourcing providers. The collaborative OSOCOS program provides a "unique value proposition" from Steria to CFS, which other outsourcing providers to CFS have not yet matched. Steria has distinguished itself as an outsourcing provider at CFS through the OSOCOS program. It is able to align with and support the Co-operative's community priorities and in doing so builds strong identification-based trust,[10] which becomes a unique value proposition in the outsourcing relationship. As a basic requirement, Steria must be able to provide IT outsourcing services to contract at a competitive price, similar to other providers at CFS. By adding a "social dimension to its value proposition" with the OSOCOS program, Steria distinguishes its services from the competition. The social impact of providing educational support to underprivileged children in India becomes integral to Steria's overall strategy and to the continuation of its outsourcing relationship with CFS.

Management lessons: Sustainability collaboration

Table 4.2 lists the five management lessons that we can glean from the Steria–CFS case, for sustainability in the outsourcing relationship. Each management lesson is described in more detail on the following pages.

Table 4.2 Five management lessons from the Steria–CFS case

- Collaborative sustainability builds trust and improves communication between buyer and provider staff
- Collaborative sustainability inspires people: attracts and retains employees and inspires commitment to work longer and harder.
- Leaders in sustainability benefit from the halo effect: CFS is able to attract the attention of providers that would normally seek out larger clients
- Sustainability is not an optional extra: sustainability has become a required business competency in outsourcing RFPs, bids and contracts; it is something to measure, and it should be measured
- Addressing the outsourcing paradox: firms need to reduce costs and still maintain social responsibility to stakeholders

Lesson 1: Collaborative sustainability builds trust and improves communication

The most important lesson that emerges from the Steria–CFS relationship is the opportunity to build trust in the outsourcing relationship by collaborating on sustainability projects. As described in Chapter 3, trust between outsourcing provider and buyer is important to building a successful relationship. The first level, calculus-based trust, is reflected in the outsourcing contract where rewards and penalties are defined and calculated. However, identification-based trust where "each party effectively understands, agrees with, empathizes with and takes each other's values"[11] aptly describes the OSOCOS collaboration. A CFS executive told us about the desired relationship with outsourcing providers: "We want a common set of values – to build more trust, [with] like-minded organizations, [where] we share something in common."

Collaborative sustainability helps the provider to better understand the buyer and allows the relationship to develop beyond the commercial contract of the outsourcing relationship. Collaboration on sustainability projects creates contexts and circumstances in which greater trust can be built between the outsourcing provider and buyer, which takes the relationship between the two parties beyond the service-level agreements expressed in the contract. As one Steria executive said:

These trips out to India are where you really get to know your customers, because you're with them 24 hours a day. And when you share different experiences with them, as you know, it puts your relationship on a very different plain. I think the closer that you work together, the more effective you are. And then from my point of view, the more effective you are, you keep the business.

Figures 4.7 and 4.8 depict the relationships between employees within CFS and Steria. Figure 4.7 shows the internal hierarchical reporting relationships within each firm, and the outsourcing contractual and relationship management linkage. Figure 4.8 provides a view of the relationships between CFS and Steria collaboration on the OSOCOS project. The collaboration provides an opportunity for much greater interaction and cross-linkage between the people in the two firms beyond that of the formal communication routes detailed in the outsourcing contract. This greater breadth of communication increases the opportunity for improving the relationship between CFS and Steria beyond the contractual outsourcing foundation and at multiple levels within each organization. It also cuts across the formal hierarchy for problem solving or when things go wrong.

A Steria manager said "[sustainability] initiatives have helped to diminish the formal communication hierarchy – allows more junior staff to speak directly with seniors on a [sustainability] related activity". Furthermore, a CFS executive told us that "the [Steria staff and executives] are closer to the action. They are closer to the internal discussion. It's not a standoff

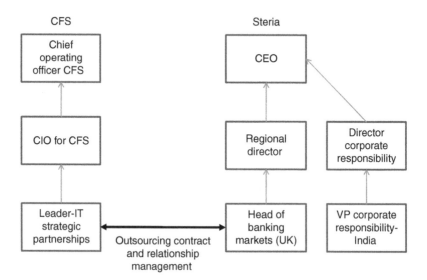

Figure 4.7 Internal reporting relationships and outsourcing relationship
Source: Steria, CFS management interviews.

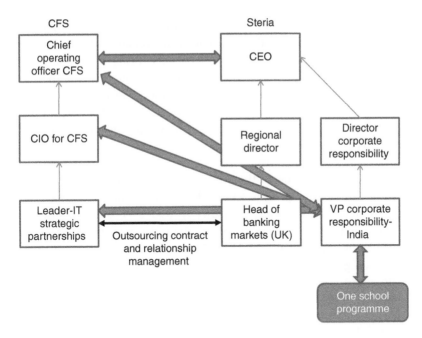

Figure 4.8 Inter-firm sustainability relationships
Source: Steria, CFS management interviews.

where "I'm protecting my IP mindset". So the defenses go down and as a result of that other things open. They participate in the charity event. They participate in the general spirit and culture of things that are happening".

The buyer and provider "harmonize" as people begin to develop a collective identity (their defenses go down) and to empathize strongly with each other. Trust develops through regular communication and watching each other perform in social situations, experiencing a variety of emotional states and learning how others view this behavior.[12] One Steria executive commenting on OSOCOS project's benefits said: "It's about working with my main contacts; working with India enables me to understand what makes CFS tick, what makes the company tick." As another Steria executive noted,

> I would just say it massively helps with our relationship and how we work together, you also bring in teamwork and there's so many other things that come into it, other skills such as communication. You really get to know the people who you're working with, and when you see them out of a techie environment, it makes a huge difference.

This last quote shows the importance of team building and the importance of "getting to know each other" outside of the formal work environment; to understand the person outside of the outsourcing relationship. This comment typifies the Steria–CFS relationship, where the interpersonal relationship is considered to be equally as important as the contractual relationship. The value of a higher level of trust is that it delivers additional benefits, such as when things don't go well in a project delivery. As a Steria executive observes:

> So when you've been to these places and shared the experience with people, it does help form a very close relationship...Let's face it, in outsourcing things don't go perfectly well over time because they don't and that's the reality of it. You're in a world where you're delivering projects and services. It's a fast moving world and not all projects go perfectly well. Good relationships get you through on those situations...you keep the buyers that you have, and that's about strong relationships.

This comment strongly echoes other research besides our own on the importance of trust in outsourcing projects, "which frequently require the cooperation of strangers in tough, high-stress situations".[13] Trust develops through a "frame-change", in this case the collaboration in India, in which the CFS and Steria employees have moved to a personal identification with each other. Besides OSOCOS project, CFS invites outsourcing providers to its community day activities, as described by one CFS executive:

> Because it's a team-building exercise as well...we are trying to involve each other in those types of activity because it helps to embed the relationship in a way that just meeting around the table in the office doesn't do.... It helps to embed the relationship and just make people feel like they are one community.

This sense of collective identity, shared goals and values echoes what we heard at Rio Tinto in Chapter 2 where the concept of shared values and cultural fit were seen to be important characteristics, especially when outsourcing involves services and prices that are fairly similar between competing providers.

Lesson 2: Collaborative sustainability inspires people

There are many examples of how sustainability initiatives can inspire people and encourage improved productivity, for both the buyer and the provider. There are two points of key interest here: first, collaboration on the OSOCOS project was seen to reduce employee attrition/turnover. Second, the collaboration was seen to build engagement, team work and, ultimately, increased productivity at work. Both of these points are a by-product of trust.

Let us first make sense of why collaboration on sustainability projects has contributed to lower staff turnover. CFS recognizes and values the low turnover of the Steria outsourcing employees. Managing staff turnover is a perennial problem in outsourcing. According to one Steria executive,

> Turnover is the biggest thing for me. So we're not constantly losing staff in their area and bringing new staff in and letting it just start off with new skills, which means projects have more of a success of delivery in the time schedule set.

The Steria average attrition rate for 2010 was 16.5%, whereas attrition on the CFS project was 12% and in some cases Steria turnover could be as high as 25%. Others have reported that Indian outsourcing providers "can expect to lose 15 to 20 percent of their work forces each year".[14] Turnover is costly for the provider, who must hire and train new replacement employees, and can be problematic for buyers because of the disruption to service when a provider staff member leaves. Reducing attrition is a benefit to both the outsourcing provider and buyer because the buyer gains continuous service from a knowledgeable outsourcing employee and the provider keeps training and recruiting costs low. Steria reported in 2010 that its average annual training cost is €691 per person, and the number of annual average days of training is 2.7 days per person. CFS spent more than £32 million on outsourcing with Steria in 2009, which suggests that there are several hundred Steria employees working on the CFS account. The ability to reduce attrition by 4.5% from the organization average should translate into significant savings for Steria.

Steria executives commented that the Indian outsourcing market has a high level of employee turnover. We heard from one Steria executive about the challenges of keeping turnover low:

> India [is] going through huge attrition throughout each outsourcer – it doesn't matter whether it's BPO, ITO. There is massive attrition because the labor pool is becoming far more switched-on and they are moving to that extra three rupees or the promise of a different kind of

education... India is booming again this year. And attrition is a massive issue for the industry... attrition on the CFS account is really, really... nothing compared to others, I mean it stands out... what it is certainly linked to is the strength of the relationship between the two organizations which is really visible to the guys in India... you couldn't say the reason for the low attrition on CFS is because what we do on CSR. But it's certainly part of the equation... definitely a factor.

Turnover in India has become a critical topic in the outsourcing industry, with associated costs and service quality issues that are important for both provider and buyer.

A Steria executive described the lower staff attrition on the CFS account but cautioned that it was not entirely attributable to the OSOCOS project:

> We do have a lower attrition rate on the CFS account, I don't think it's purely down to OSOCOS but I think it contributes. The ethical and social element does help. I wouldn't say it was THE reason why the attrition rate is lower but it definitely contributes.

Although sustainability cannot be pinpointed as the only factor, anything that lowers staff turnover is a benefit to the buyer and the provider. In an outsourcing relationship, where the service is delivered by well-trained and experienced staff, lower attrition, which reduces costs and improves service, is a major benefit. The benefit may be considered strategic if the cause of the lower attrition is unique and not easily replicated by another provider. The reduced staff attrition between CFS and Steria, which is partially attributed to collaborative sustainability, would be difficult for another provider to quickly reproduce, given the time and energy required to create the initial collaboration between the two firms.

The second main area of benefit is in the form of a more highly motivated, more engaged group of employees at both Steria and CFS. This is because the employees have a sense that they are working toward an inspiring vision that is about more than just being profitable. The CFS annual report states the aim "to build a better society... to be an ethical leader; to be an exemplary employer". In a period when global financial challenges have disrupted many national economies, this vision, which is demonstrated through sustainability projects, motivates employees. A senior manager at CFS told us how the sustainability projects motivated the employees:

It's the fact that we've got thousands [of] people sitting down at lunch with each other talking about this stuff...engagement is the issue for me. If I've got engaged staff, they're going to stand up and step forward rather than sit back and be passive. I mean it's not just in the textbook, it's a fact you see. It's exudes from the pores of the individuals working on a program...engagement is the thing.

One CFS senior manager told us about the engagement benefit of OSOCOS:

I have people that come back happier, much more engaged, and feel they're actually doing something which fits in with the values of the companies. So I think the staff engagement, that's just a great thing to do upfront...I see direct and immediate benefit there...they're coming back and they write blogs on it. So they write on blogs on what they saw – you know the children that they met, what they are saying.

Productivity is a key benefit from motivated and engaged employees. Employees at CFS and at Steria who are inspired by a working environment with a vision that is more than simply growing profits tended to work longer and with more dedication. Interviewees spoke of the energy and attentiveness of the motivated employees who are engaged in sustainability projects between Steria and CFS. One Steria account manager told us that *"People stay longer, sometimes they're investing a lot of their time and it's not paid, I won't necessarily see it on my bottom line, but you will see it on the productiveness of that project, of hitting targets, etc."* A CFS executive, when discussing the motivation of Steria employees who value the strength of the relationship with CFS, said:

when you are under pressure of getting the tests done against a tight deadline, do you know what the guys say? Well, time to go home now, or do they stay for midnight? These guys stay until midnight and beyond and all night if necessary...the school [sustainability] thing is just a little part of that – it just builds that.

This demonstrates the benefits of shared values where the Steria employees have developed a collective identity with CFS and have committed to commonly shared values such as helping schools with needy children in India rewarded by working late to complete an important software project. Other researchers have described similar phenomenon of employee engagement though social responsibility. Researcher Timothy Bowman describes the intensifying search for meaning and purpose in work...and that employees are looking to business to answer questions about the meaning of life" and "employees are looking for a sense of connectedness or community at work, and for their work to be an opportunity to contribute towards society.[15]

Others have described how social responsibility in the workplace boosts employee engagement, suggesting that "a sense of pride [from social responsibility] is a major driver of both morale and results...Companies that enhance their reputations through sustainability perform better, and generate greater employee loyalty from workers."[16] There is nothing necessarily new about motivated employees being more productive. What is new in this research is that outsourcing provider and buyer employees working together, on sustainability projects that they all support, contributes to improving the trust between the two groups and enables them to collectively become more motivated and productive in their outsourcing work.

Lesson 3: Leaders in sustainability benefit from the "halo effect"

The position of CFS as a sustainability leader enables it to attract outsourcing providers that may not otherwise be interested in this mid-sized financial services customer due to a knock-on "halo effect" that results from CFS being associated with the positive attributes of sustainability. CFS is able to work with outsourcing providers to co-develop their brands and reputation regarding sustainability. The MIT Sustainability Initiative has identified sustainability as an important issue that affects the management of all organizations. The research suggests that "sustainability will have an increasingly large impact on the business landscape going forward....First movers are likely to gain a commanding lead; it may be increasingly difficult for competitors to catch up."[17] CFS is a leader in sustainability, as evidenced by its policies, awards, the contents of the sustainability report and its long history of social responsibility.

First, CFS' reputation attracts leading providers who want to be associated with a sustainability leader. Interviewees called this the "halo effect", whereby providers' sustainability reputation benefits by association with CFS. This benefits CFS by attracting better qualified providers. Second, by working with CFS on sustainability projects, the providers and CFS co-develop their brands, thereby reinforcing each other's sustainability reputation. As one CFS executive suggested, "They see being associated with CFS or Co-op Group as a positive from a branding perspective. Our brand already carries certain amount of weight from an ethical [sustainability] perspective."

As one CFS employee stated,

> "we punch above our weight" when attracting global provider. We get a much better team from these providers than we deserve for the size of organization and the business we're doing with them ... It's because of the name and the halo effect and the fact that they want to do business ... they are all overly keen to do business with us, overly keen. For the size we are and the money we spend with them, it doesn't stack up. But they don't want to go anywhere without having the Co-op as a brand on their list of customers.

Sustainability leadership currently is an advantage for CFS, but this may not offer an enduring benefit as other organizations seek to emulate CFS' sustainability reputation. Currently, this reputation allows CFS to attract and work with leading outsourcing providers and receive a higher level of quality service than they might otherwise receive.

Providers want to benefit from the association with one of the leading UK sustainability organizations because they increasingly recognize the importance of sustainability to their employees, customers and other stakeholders. Providers work in a highly competitive global market where a distinctive capability such as sustainability can help them be more successful in winning outsourcing business.

One CFS manager responsible for commercial outsourcing relations told us: "They are looking to partner with us on a community project where we invest, they invest and we both put our name on it. They see being associated with CFS or Co-op group as a positive from a branding perspective." He commented that improved branding through the halo effect will "help them get some new business". "Once five people turn up with pretty much identical software, and you can negotiate the prices, what's going to make the difference, and I could see something like [sustainability] making a difference." The last comment is interesting, in that some parts of the outsourcing market have become commoditized, such as hardware and some application software. Outsourcing providers increasingly look for a capability that distinguishes their services or products from the competition, especially when prices are similar. CFS also works to influence providers. As a CFS manager told us: "We seek to influence suppliers to live up to our standards; we are that much further advanced."

Lesson 4: Sustainability is not an "optional extra"

Sustainability has become a required competency in outsourcing. Buyers such as CFS will expect that outsourcing providers are able to demonstrate basic sustainability qualifications. For example, at CFS all potential providers are required to pass an ethical assessment performed by an outside firm. This is the minimum sustainability requirement for a provider. CFS prides itself on the fact that it has turned away suppliers (and profitable lending business) because of ethical considerations. For example, one provider was acquired by an organization with operations in military equipment and armament. CFS severed ties with the firm because it failed the ethical assessment. All suppliers must comply with the CFS Sustainable Procurement and Supplier Policy (SPSP). As one CFS executive stated,

> They have to fit in, as part of the criteria, when we do any RFIs [Requests for Information] or RFPs. It's a big measuring stick for these third parties and actually if we find something that we're not comfortable with, we won't even do business with them ... There's a bar they have to get over and if you don't get over it, we can't do business with them.

The providers have seen an increased requirement for sustainability in RFPs from all buyers, not just at CFS. As one Steria executive stated,

> ... absolutely in every bid now without exception. I have not seen a bid in the last two years where it's not covered. Sometimes it's covered in more depth ... it's always in there now. Five years ago it was not there at all, it's emerged over the last five years. In every bid it's a big thing. It's now into the kind of environment stuff as well, which we're starting to see. That's only very recently we are seeing this.

Some providers will extol their sustainability qualifications through marketing and communications. Recognizing the growing importance of sustainability, many providers will "bolt-on" an inauthentic image of sustainability, a claim without evidence. For purposes of definition, we describe "authentic sustainability" as a set of sustainability activities and projects that have a substantial tangible impact on society and/or the environment. In contrast to this, "inauthentic sustainability" activities are sustainability activities or projects that have insubstantial or intangible impact on society and/or the environment. Inauthentic sustainability is often marked with hyperbole in marketing communication.

Employees at CFS and Steria were skeptical of the recent surge in provider firms adopting sustainability as though it were tags or "badges" that are quickly worn and easily changed. CFS is proud of its long history, and many interviewees spoke of sustainability as "part of our DNA, the ethos of the Co-op" and "it's the right thing to do". Some CFS interviewees spoke of the need to embrace sustainability as a social obligation, and not strictly as a commercial position. As one CFS interviewee stated,

> where other businesses do [sustainability] for commercial advantage and if they didn't get any commercial advantage from doing it, they wouldn't do it, we [at CFS] do it because it's the right thing to do, oh and by the way it may well give us a commercial advantage.

From one CFS executive:

> I see too many UK companies who move into this space, as doing it solely for the purpose of brand enhancement, and therefore I have doubts in their motives and sincerity behind it. So, when the pressure comes on I could see it stopping.

An outsourcing provider executive, speaking of a former outsourcing employer stated: "as an example, they talk about sustainability. I never really saw any of that in the two years I was working there. So I read about it, heard about it, but never saw anything in action."

The most telling example was the personal commitment of CFS senior executives to sustainability, as evidenced by stories about personal time spent traveling to India and even personal financial commitment to the OSOCOS project by those executives. According to a senior outsourcing manager at CFS,

> "I know that [the CIO's] commitment is genuine and it takes time... More cynical firms would always pick the visible things. You'd always pick the high profile things. You try to choose the things that would give you the quick wins... but it doesn't work."

Lesson 5: Addressing the outsourcing paradox

Global outsourcing is controversial and some commentators have forcefully argued that it is detrimental to social responsibility.[18] GITO engagement may be seen as counter to the Co-operative's formally stated social responsibility to communities. CFS work is now performed in India, which may result in job loss or redeployment in its home country. Since CFS is working with Steria to improve the lives of underprivileged children in India, the Co-operative's social responsibility reputation may remain intact so that the Co-operative's goal "to do so much more than create profit" continues to be legitimate. Here we confront the paradox of social responsibility in outsourcing, where the organization seeks to protect its workers and their communities with ongoing employment, while providing services to its customers at a competitive cost. One CFS executive said, "It's almost a bit like the 'mad auntie' in the cupboard, we all know she's there but we don't talk about her." When asked directly, however, several CFS executives were straightforward about the paradox:

> "We will not outsource our front office; but given our scale, we cannot take advantage of cost efficiencies of outsourcing the back office. We are simply not big enough to buck the market" "if you didn't offshore your back office you wouldn't have a front office". "For many businesses, if they don't go down that path [of outsourcing] they won't exist, and there will be bigger job losses."
>
> You're not going to stop this [global outsourcing]. [India] is the commodity side of IT, the center of the world. They can do it better than us, they can do it faster than us, they can do it cheaper than us. So what are we going to do? Are we going to ignore it, are we going to go bust while all of these other people use them? We can't be socially responsible if we don't have money to invest in social responsibility.

This theme identifies the delicate balance that CFS and other outsourcing buyers must manage to maintain the trust of their workers and customers. Both of these stakeholder groups may be opposed to offshore outsourcing, as jobs and employment move away from the communities where CFS operates. CFS executives must carefully determine the amount of outsourcing that will reduce costs sufficiently to remain competitive, while not alienating customers and workers. The OSOCOS project alleviates some of the concern that the CFS outsourcing action is done only to improve profits and mitigates the action of moving local jobs offshore.

From a legal perspective, CFS outsourcing contracts offer examples of social responsibility practices in outsourcing. Outsourced workers may not be moved beyond a certain radius of kilometers from their original workplace. Another example is an outsourcing deal that failed to move ahead because the provider would not accept the sustainable procurement and supplier policy provision for collective bargaining.

Some CFS executives suggested that outsourcing work can have an upside for global society. One CFS executive told us,

"It's a balance that we must strike between showing commitment to this country and also developing other economies, which is ultimately in our interests; we are a global economy." ... "We should be a global organization." "Everybody that works on the account [in India], if you go and talk to them, they go on and look after 20, 30 people with the pay they get ... It betters the lives of the whole family."

Several interviewees stressed the need to balance goals for sustainability and the goals for commercial success. One manager told us,

We are all commercial organizations that at the bottom line we want to do it the right way. We want to do ethically. We want to do it sustainably, but we do have to make a profit.

Conclusion

Figure 4.9 depicts the five management lessons from the CFS–Steria case aligned with the Porter and Kramer model. Clearly, buyers and providers should embrace the opportunities that sustainability brings to the outsourcing relationship. The top three lessons certainly align with the strategic perspective that Porter and Kramer describe, as philanthropy has leveraged capability and improved salient parts of the competitive context for both Steria and CFS. The fourth lesson states that sustainability

Figure 4.9 Lessons from CFS–Steria linked to responsive-strategic concepts
Source: Steria, CFS management interviews; Porter and Kramer (2006).

is no longer an optional extra for most organizations that must respond to stakeholder expectations in today's markets and societies. The fifth lesson is a foundational theme that is quite unique to outsourcing, which suggests that the outsourcing buyer must address the issue of moving work (and jobs) to different locations outside of the organization and often outside the country. By embracing sustainability throughout the full outsourcing relationship, buyers and providers have a solid case to address the outsourcing paradox.

Sustainability has become a key facet of outsourcing, whether of IT or of business processes, onshore or offshore. Chapters 1, 2 and 3 have shown why the CEO should care about sustainability in outsourcing. The case of CFS and Steria shows how they have managed the collaboration on a sustainability project and created a "win-win" scenario, referred to by sustainable outsourcing researchers as "shared value".[19] The case demonstrates that sustainability has progressed beyond philanthropy to offering a business case for its integration into outsourcing arrangements. The Indian schools have benefited from the injection of resource and support; both buyer and provider have benefited from improved communication and trust, all of which has had tangible benefits. Buyer and provider benefited from the productivity and lower attrition. CFS is able to mitigate the downside of outsourcing in line with its sustainability imperatives. Collaboration with CFS offers a competitive advantage to Steria to distinguish its commodity service in a marketplace where there is limited scope for differentiation. It also presents barriers to entry for rivals bidding for the renewal of CFS contracts in the future, and thus participation in OSOCOS project "ties in" the relationship. The challenge for the CEO is knowing when to apply these practices. We will approach this topic next, in Chapter 5.

5
Leveraging Sustainability in Relationships

> Every RFP has a CSR component... Is outsourcing done to avoid corporate social responsibility? No, it is just new to this decision.
>
> Legal expert in outsourcing

As Chapter 4 showed, sustainability in outsourcing offers shared value to buyer, provider and good causes. These benefits can be strategic in the sense that competitive advantage may be derived for the buyer and provider. For example, by instilling sustainability practices throughout its operations and encouraging them at its clients, Steria gains value through reduced attrition in its workforce, thus lowering operating costs and building a trust relationship with clients that encourages further outsourcing contracts. Steria's vice president for corporate responsibility commented that "this model is feasible for any client; it can be just computer support or can be the entire model, the full client partnership". Accenture's work in India, described in Chapter 3, demonstrates that other outsourcing providers understand the benefits of collaborative sustainability.

This chapter addresses a key challenge faced by CEOs: how can buyers and providers design collaborative sustainability activities for shared value? Structured as a practice chapter, here we present a model for applying collaborative sustainability built around the research findings and relevant management theory discussed in Chapters 2, 3 and 4. The first section of this chapter addresses the "why, when and how" of sustainable collaboration between outsourcing buyers and providers and identifies three building blocks of sustainability collaboration. The second section provides a conceptual framework for collaborative sustainability in outsourcing with practical guidance on how providers and buyers should work together.

Three building blocks to sustainability collaboration

Some reasons to consider working with outsourcing providers on sustainability projects are shown in Table 5.1

These reasons are supported by case studies in earlier chapters. However, simply declaring that buyer and provider are to work collaboratively on sustainability will not create these benefits. Examining the building blocks required to establish such relationships will help us get our answer to the questions of when and with whom to engage in sustainability collaboration projects. The three key components of a sustainability relationship are the following:

- relationship maturity;
- personal interaction; and
- choosing a mutually beneficial type of proposed collaboration.

Together these building blocks are the model to guide our understanding of collaborative sustainability in a GITO relationship.

Relationship maturity

A wealth of literature shows that outsourcing relationships require time and commitment to develop.[1] A mature relationship that has developed over time provides a more fertile environment for collaboration in sustainability projects. For example, an outsourcing provider who has just begun a contract with a buyer needs to demonstrate the ability to provide the contracted service. At CFS, they call this the "hygiene factor"; the provider must be able to do what they said they would do. As we heard from one CFS executive:

> When you start off on a partnership, you don't create it overnight. As you get more into the relationship and the trust starts to build, this [collaborative sustainability] can be a very reinforcing factor. There is a timing to it. Probably, you wouldn't be doing it on day one or the first week or first month, you wouldn't be saying, "Alright, let's work together on joint community planning." It's something that would come probably a little bit later.

On the other hand, the passage of time is not a guarantee of a mature relationship. The CFS IT supplier segmentation analysis identifies four categories of suppliers: transactional, volume, essential and strategic.

Table 5.1   Reasons for sustainability collaboration

Key reason	Benefit to provider	Benefit to buyer	Benefit to both
Collaborative sustainability activities build trust and improve communication between buyer and provider in a long-term outsourcing relationship	Additional relationship tie in to improve chances of follow-on outsourcing contracts and renewals	Can ask for "extras" from provider without being charged for every activity	Ability to work through tough and unexpected problems. Builds informal communications in addition to the formal communication routes
Collaborative sustainability activity has workforce benefits: reduces attrition, inspires commitment to work longer and harder, attracts workers	Lower operating costs (training, replacement)	Retention of knowledge, reduced start-up costs, fewer errors	Overall lower costs, improved ability to attract good talent
Sustainability leaders create a halo effect	Serving a respected sustainability leader improves reputation	Attention from key suppliers, "punch above our weight"	
The outsourcing paradox – reduce costs and retain social responsibility to labor force; the tension between sustainability and commercial requirements			Recognition that both parties must have a commercially successful reputation and that the negative social issues of outsourcing need to be balanced with positive sustainability issues

Transactional products or services (e.g. personal computer maintenance) where business criticality is low may have a long-term and high-volume relationship. However, such providers may never reach the relationship maturity needed to become an essential or strategic supplier, with whom collaboration on sustainability projects would be appropriate.

The buyer and provider organizations regarded as essential or strategic can begin to work together once they have confirmed alignment on shared values, a critical step demonstrated in Chapter 2 in the Enbridge and Rio Tinto cases as well as in Chapter 4 in the Steria–CFS case. From the outsourcing buyer's perspective, CFS looks for providers who share its commitment to sustainability and expects to build long-term relationships with them. The principles for this are enacted in CFS' Sustainable Procurement and Supplier Policy. CFS will sever relationships with providers who are not able to adhere to its ethical sourcing policies. For example, it severed its contract with a software supplier that was acquired by a military arms producer, an activity that conflicted with CFS' standards. By contrast, a CFS executive described its strategic relationship with Steria by saying, "They know us inside out. They know all about the Co-op and its ethics and its values and they line up to them."

Another CFS executive explained that a strategic relationship is "when you are an integral part of the business, so the kind of work that we do is on the project side we're actually developing, we're building, we're maintaining, and it's not just a piece of software we're doing; it's a project that involves the whole business".

In reference to transactional relationships, the same manager said that "when you're developing the software and anyone can pick up the software, plug it in and use it, then partnership and trust between buyer and provider is less important".

The upshot of all this is that collaborative sustainability should be applied in relationships where trust development is important. A Steria executive explains this succinctly:

> Some are buying a transactional relationship where they want it nice and simple; we want that project or we want that box from you or whatever...and that's it. That's one end of the spectrum of outsourcing. At the other end of the spectrum, you've got a genuine partnership where there's a kind of mutual commitment to each other. You're trying to create win-win type scenarios. You both win or both fail together. And things will go wrong and you work through them.

To help in identifying appropriate suppliers and relationships for collaborative sustainability, Table 5.2 distinguishes between some features of an immature and a mature outsourcing relationship.

Personal interaction

The second consideration in deciding on sustainability collaboration is linked to the level of personal interaction, which can be characterized as

Table 5.2   Defining relationship maturity

Immature relationship	Mature relationship
Short-term, unknown relationship duration; project-focused	Several years of experience, long-term contract
Low volume of business	High volume of business
Limited business criticality	Business critical services or products
Starting to demonstrate reliable delivery of products or services	Established record of reliable delivery

low-touch or high-touch. Low-touch outsource activities require little or no personal interaction; for example disaster recovery services, data center operations or document scanning services may be completely automated, even though the service may be business-critical and high-value. High-touch activities, on the other hand, such as business process re-engineering or application implementation, require a high degree of interaction at various levels between the buyer and provider organization. In some cases, multiple organizations may be involved. Management at CFS emphasized that collaborative sustainability will not fit all outsourcing relationships. For buyer and provider to benefit from collaborative sustainability, the outsourcing arrangement must have a high amount of human interaction in order to deepen trust. As evidence of the need for a high amount of human interaction to develop growing levels of trust, one CFS executive described a high-touch situation, saying:

> the [outsourcing] relationship is application development, which means you're running projects; a project is very much about people working together to deliver something...so it isn't transactional...by its very nature you do need a more communicative relationship...you have to communicate. You have to build the relationship in order to deliver effectively; so I think the very nature of what we're wanting to get out of it requires it to be managed in a certain way.

Some outsourcing relationships do not require a high amount of human interaction, and trust is not required beyond the contractual controls. For example, when data center, hardware support or telecommunications resources are outsourced there are relatively lower levels of buyer–provider personal interactions than that would be required in a major application development project. When human interaction is minimal, such as in automated data backup and recovery services, the concepts of increased

Table 5.3   Levels of personal interaction

Low touch – Low personal interaction – poor choice for collaborative sustainability	High touch – High personal interaction – good choice for collaborative sustainability
Technology-based service or product	High service-level requirement, low technology component to service
Limited communication between buyer and provider after contract	High level of communication required for project to be successful
Can be delivered from a distance (off-shored) with limited need for in-person meetings	On-site interaction frequently required, for governance, planning, requirements, review, discussion, etc.

trust are less applicable and the benefits of collaborative sustainability would be difficult to derive. In short, building trust relies on interaction between people, and limited interaction will diminish the opportunity for its development.

Table 5.3 provides a set of characteristics of low-touch and high-touch aspects of the personal interaction concept.

Type of sustainability collaboration

The third consideration is the type of sustainability collaboration. This is the ability of the two organizations to identify and work together on sustainability initiatives that are beneficial to the relationship. For example, CFS identifies three different levels of sustainability in the relationship between the buyer and provider: hygiene, alignment and enablement.

Hygiene sustainability is the basic, minimal sustainability level that is acceptable to do business together. The provider is expected to live up to the buyers' basic sustainability expectations and provide the services reliably at a competitive price. At CFS, this means that the provider has passed the ethics review required for all suppliers. The Co-operative's Sustainable Procurement and Supplier Policy states that CFS will work with suppliers and partners who can make a positive contribution to its pursuit of sustainable development and identifies standards such as the Universal Declaration of Human Rights, freedom of association and collective bargaining and a safe and hygienic working environment. Jim Slack, the CIO at CFS said, "if we find something [relating to sustainability and social responsibility] that we are not comfortable with we won't even do business with them".

At the second level, alignment, providers and buyers align their sustainability priorities to focus on mutual opportunities, for example in

Table 5.4 Levels of sustainability collaboration

Sustainability level	Trust level (from Chapter 4)	Collaborative sustainability strategy
Hygiene	Calculus/contractual	Compliance with requirements (e.g. CFS SPSP) and regulations (e.g. UK Carbon Reduction Commitment)
Alignment	Knowledge-based	Support for mutually agreed projects (e.g. combined effort on local community projects)
Enablement	Identification-based	Collaborate on sustainability projects that add shared value both to the organizations and to the community (e.g. Steria and CFS' joint support for schools in India, Accenture's education program in India)

support of local charities. This alignment can support the sustainability priorities of both parties and reinforce the relationship. CFS communicates three sustainability priorities to its suppliers, which include inspiring children, reducing global climate change and reducing poverty to allow outsourcing vendors to focus on topics that are important.

The third level of sustainability collaboration is enablement: the outsourcing buyer and supplier, working perhaps with a third party such as a charitable foundation, NGO or community organization, combine forces to create a new capability that would be beyond that of each individual organization. For example, the Rockefeller Foundation has focused on outsourcing as a mechanism to "generate a step-function income improvement for those at the base of the pyramid ... [who benefit from] ... sustainable employment as principle workers in business process outsourcing centers".[2] At this level, both organizations benefit from the collaboration and they make a contribution to the society. This creates shared value, "which involves creating economic value [outsourcing] in a way that also creates value for society by addressing its needs and challenges" (Table 5.4).[3]

A framework for collaborative sustainability in outsourcing

Figure 5.1 shows a matrix to help us visually conceptualize the relationship between the three building blocks discussed above. The ability of an outsourcing provider and buyer to collaborate on sustainability is related

	Low touch	High touch
Immature	A. Hygiene	B. Alignment to enablement
Mature	C. Hygiene to alignment	D. Enablement

Figure 5.1 Collaborative sustainability quadrants

to the maturity of the relationship, the degree of personal interaction needed in the relationship and the level of sustainability actions to be implemented. As a guide, outsourcing buyers and providers should only try to engage in enablement-type collaborative sustainability in relationships that have already matured or where greater maturity is desirable (quadrant B to D), and where the work that is outsourced requires high-touch (quadrant D). If a high-touch service is outsourced but the relationship is immature (quadrant B), then alignment activities should be in place and plans made for enablement collaboration. If personal interaction is low-touch, then the opportunity for benefits to accrue from enablement-type sustainability, collaboration is low anyway, so here it would be reasonable to maintain hygiene sustainability.

Figure 5.2 is an example of provider positioning in the framework. Outsourcing provider A is relatively immature in the relationship and may

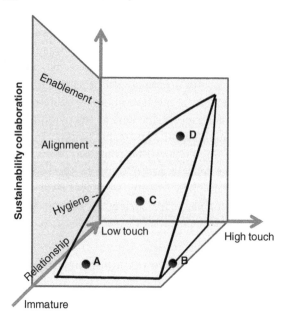

Figure 5.2 Examples of collaboration sustainability in GITO

provide a service that is not seen as critical at the time. In addition, the service is seen as low-touch, requiring limited personal interactions.

For this provider, aside from meeting the basic hygiene sustainability, there is no benefit to be obtained from engaging with the buyer in collaborative sustainability activities. On the other hand, provider B has a relationship that is at the same maturity stage as provider A but delivers a high-touch service requiring substantial personal interaction. Provider B is in a much better position to move to higher levels of sustainability activity with the buyer. Providers A and B should display hygiene sustainability but will not yet be able to attain the enablement sustainability level with the buyer.

Provider C may not have the same level of personal interaction as that of provider B but has developed a more mature relationship, perhaps with the passage of time, or perhaps because of the volume and criticality of business conducted with the buyer.

Finally, provider D is at the highest level of sustainability collaboration, with a high-touch service at the same level as provider B, but with a more mature relationship that qualifies for discussions on enablement sustainability collaboration. Provider D has earned the right to collaborate with the buyer on sustainability initiatives. This is not a one-sided relationship; the buyer may actively pull the provider toward that level as well, because both can benefit from sustainability collaboration. For example, as described in the Steria–CFS case, by working closely together on sustainability initiatives, the relationship is developed, trust is built, the buyer can rely more heavily on the provider in tough times and the provider can expect a longer and more fruitful commercial relationship. Employee turnover in this relationship may be lowered to the benefit of both provider and buyer.

In contrast, provider relationships such as those illustrated by position A or B may never reach a state where they can engage in substantive sustainability collaboration. Some outsourcing providers will deliver services and develop relationships that are unsuited for this type of discussion. Both the buyer and the provider should recognize this reality and should at a minimum agree to hygiene or alignment sustainability, such as supporting agreed charitable causes with financial contributions. Indeed, these are the positions where sustainability activity for marketing or branding purposes may be seen as artificial. Buyers who determine that a provider is "greenwashing" may react more negatively to that provider than to one who honestly admits that sustainability is not a critical factor in its service delivery, aside from the mandatory hygiene factors. Figure 5.3 depicts this example in position F, where the provider has a high-touch service and

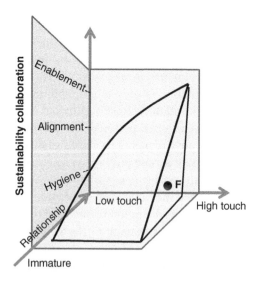

Figure 5.3 Example of non-collaboration sustainability in GITO

a mature relationship but has no interest in collaboration on sustainable activities. Hygiene sustainability should remain, but the enablement stage will not be pursued.

Action planning for managers

From the perspective of an outsourcing buyer, a four-step action plan for engaging in collaborative sustainability might proceed as described below:

1) Recognize appropriate providers;
2) Focus on common initiatives;
3) Start small and grow incrementally; and
4) Measure, revise and reconfirm.

First, recognize those outsourcing providers who have earned the right to collaborate, as discussed above. Typically, these will be strategic providers who have a large outsourcing contract for critical services, with a high degree of human interaction. Providers would be assessed in terms of the type of service, the maturity of the relationship and the compatibility of values and sustainability priorities. Not all outsourcing providers will be receptive to collaborative sustainability. Some will prefer to operate with the simpler voluntary philanthropy with no need to collaborate with buyers. For example, another GITO provider also provides critical, high-value services for CFS. This provider has a very strong sustainability profile, but we could find no examples of collaborative sustainability in the relationship between CFS and this provider. Currently, this provider prefers to maintain the voluntary philanthropy model and focus its sustainability efforts in-house. The relationship between buyer and provider is not yet mature, and trust is still contractual (calculus-based), so that both sides are not yet amenable to pursuing a relationship of collaborative sustainability.

Second, focus on sustainability initiatives that are common, or that are considered by both organizations to be priorities. Both parties should look for sustainability issues that they agree are on their list of priorities. For example, both CFS and Steria have identified the education of young people as a priority. CFS has identified climate change, and Steria has begun to implement solar power in its school program, which presents a new opportunity for collaboration. The outsourcing buyer and provider should constantly review and refresh their sustainability priorities and opportunities, as determined by their individual corporate priorities and as new opportunities become available. Shared value requires a need for "an ongoing exploration of societal needs [which] will lead companies to discover new opportunities for differentiation and repositioning in traditional markets, and to recognize the potential of new markets they previously overlooked".[4]

Third, start with small collaborative sustainability initiatives. In the Steria–CFS case study, a single school in India became the starting point for a potentially larger network of schools; at the time of our case study two schools were involved. The message to managers is to start small, with a large vision, and grow the initiative over time. This allows managers to learn from mistakes and to disengage if the relationship fails.

Fourth, measure and revise the collaborative efforts and reconfirm that ongoing sustainability projects continue to meet objectives for the individual organizations and for the outsourcing relationship. For example, Chicago-based financial services provider Northern Trust has used the balanced scorecard measure to compare its sustainability collaboration with important outsourcing providers. The scorecard approach recognizes the need to build in a timeframe for the collaboration projects.

Case 5.1: Collaborative sustainability at Northern Trust

Northern Trust is a global wealth and asset management organization, headquartered in Chicago. The organization is proud of its 120-year history of giving back to the communities in which it operates with a strong corporate social responsibility orientation.[5]

Northern Trust has applied its CSR orientation to its outsourcing relationships. At the 2011 IAOP Global Outsourcing Summit, representatives from Northern Trust presented an overview of their model for sustainability collaboration with global IT outsourcing providers. The Northern Trust model relies on the Porter and Kramer responsive-strategic CSR framework and uses a structured approach to engage outsourcing providers. TCS is the major outsourcing provider working on collaborative sustainability with Northern Trust.

In addition to the Porter and Kramer model, Northern Trust uses the balanced scorecard to set goals and measure progress on the degree of collaboration with its outsourcing providers. Also, Northern Trust is developing a model to calculate return on investment (ROI) for CSR, looking at outcomes such as reduced workforce attrition. Importantly, Northern Trust recognizes that it must work collaboratively with its outsource partners, especially those that outsource globally, in order to have a large global impact. Many outsourcing providers are eager to partner with Northern Trust on this, and often ask "if we do this do we get the business?" The answer is "not necessarily so" as Northern Trust begins to define consistent and clear CSR and environmental sustainability expectations for its providers, much like CFS does. Completely independent from the Steria–CFS case, Northern Trust is proceeding toward an identical goal of collaboration on social and environmental topics with its key vendors.

Conclusion

The Steria–CFS outsourcing relationship is an excellent example of collaborative sustainability. Perhaps CFS is a unique case due to its organizational emphasis on sustainability and its 165-year history as a co-operative. However, sustainability is a rapidly growing topic of interest for many organizations. CFS' actions for collaborative sustainability in outsourcing make it a leader and bellwether for others to follow.

By examining the role of sustainability in outsourcing at CFS, we have provided a model for practical management action based on a recognized leader. As explained by the Steria marketing director, and as suggested by the Accenture Corporate Citizenship leader in India, this model can be replicated with different outsourcing buyers. The OSOCOS program was not unique to the CFS outsourcing arrangement. Steria has deployed the model with different buyers in different markets. For example, we learned of a similar collaborative model at the UK Royal Mail, where 2,500 hours were contributed to integrated community programs in 2010. The Steria UK marketing director told us that this type of activity distinguishes Steria in the marketplace and had been successful in helping it win new outsourcing contracts. For example, Steria won an outsourcing contract for emergency shared services in the region of Cleveland (UK) in 2010, partially through recognition of the community commitment demonstrated by its support for police activities in primary schools. The vice president for corporate responsibility in India described how several outsourcing buyers contributed to the success of the Steria One School Program. Other outsourcing buyers who participate in the Steria OSOCOS include British Telecom, Boots, Lloyds TSB and the BBC.

The right combination of outsourcing relationship maturity and personal interaction is required to initiate collaborative sustainability. For astute IT outsourcing providers, this model provides an interesting opportunity to further cement an outsourcing relationship, extending the value of the relationship and protecting it from competition. Collaborative sustainability provides a strategic capability for those providers who earn the right to engage outsourcing buyers.

Collaborative sustainability will not be appropriate for all outsourcing relationships. Our model suggests that several conditions should be in place before the concept can be considered in the relationship. However, we infer from our findings that when the conditions are in place and the outsourcing buyer and provider engage in collaborative sustainability projects, both will gain long-term benefits. These all contribute to a lower-risk, more successful outsourcing relationship, which benefits both the buyer and the provider.

The implications for outsourcing buyers are as follows:

- carefully assess where collaborative sustainability can be developed with strategic outsourcing providers and begin the discussion;
- seek alignment on sustainability values and priorities; start with initial projects and expect the provider to follow with larger activities; and
- constantly monitor and measure the progress and value of collaborative sustainability projects.

6
Steering a Course on Sustainability

Introduction

As this book has illustrated, sustainability is a key issue for all organizations and has emerged as a central dimension to the management of outsourcing, both onshore and offshore. The big question is how to integrate sustainability into outsourcing arrangements and secondly how to "do well by doing good", that is to harness pro-market strategies in order to increase returns on philanthropic investment.

This book has presented a number of cases and models, but success in managing sustainability is not about uncritically applying a cookie-cutter approach. Every situation will be contextually different and the participants' attitudes are shaped by particular historical, economic, political and/or cultural circumstances. Thus, in this chapter we suggest some mechanisms for thoughtful, reflective sustainability practice.

We have shown how buyer and provider organizations can embrace social and environmental concerns and both can benefit in shared value, leading to a "win-win" outcome. However, there has been an associated critique of this pro-market position on sustainability that questions the unrestrained involvement of capitalist organizations whose primary responsibility is to provide dividends to shareholders and/or pre-empt stricter government controls.[1] An inherent dichotomy exists between the pro-market orientation of most business entities and the sustainability expectations of society, which is this: business typically has a short-term perspective to provide economic returns to shareholders, whereas sustainability implies a limitless timeframe for all of society and the environment.

Managers walk a thin line between seeking returns from positive consumer, employee and investor perceptions of the company while avoiding the risks of negative government intervention, adverse media exposure, stock market declines and customer boycotts.[2]

Our attention up to now has been focused on the benefits to the buyer and provider with the assumption of automatic benefits for the "good cause". An example for good cause is the OSOCOS schools project in India shown in the Steria–CFS case. In this final chapter, we reflect on the third party in this arrangement and shine light on the development of the "good cause" to examine the effectiveness of this pro-market direction for sustainability and to stimulate thoughtful management action. We caution that short-term interventions in sustainability projects by outsourcing buyers and providers, although admirable, must also consider the long-term requirements for the projects to be sustainable.

Toward reflective practice in sustainability

Reflection is the practice of periodically stepping back to ponder one's self and those in one's immediate environment.[3] The object of reflection in a business context may be in three areas: first, content reflection is about how a practical problem was solved; second, process reflection examines the procedures and the sequence of the events; and third, premise reflection involves questioning the presuppositions attending the problem. The timing of reflection may be anticipatory, contemporaneous or retrospective. Originally, Donald Schön[4] characterized the work of design as a reflective

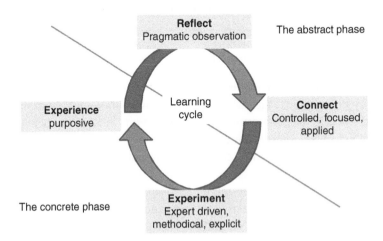

Figure 6.1　The learning cycle, applied to sustainability projects

"conversation" with the situation, which became known as "reflection-in-action". In environmental management, for example reflective practice helps environmental managers consider the implications of their specific project activities with respect to the broader context (Figure 6.1).

Case 6.1: Sustainability therapy in environmental projects in Malta

Bell and Morse[5] examined a set of environmental projects in Malta that focused on coastal area management. The key issue that the authors explored was the apparent contradiction between the project-oriented nature of sustainable development and the implied circularity of sustainability whereby there is no "end". Projects have clear parameters such as accountability, measurable impact, value for money and time-bound delivery schedules. The authors suggest a concept called sustainability therapy, which involves learning and reflective practice to achieve a broader perspective within the linear constraints of sustainability projects. They suggest a learning cycle, based on Kolb's work, which involves reflecting, connecting, modeling and then doing.

   This process allows the project stakeholders to appreciate the limits and the potentials of the project they are in and allows them to carry forward this learning into other activities. The purpose of sustainability therapy is to create reflective orientation so that the project outcomes are enduring, that is sustainable.

Viewing sustainability holistically: A complementary lens

So far our analysis has focused on GITO buyers and providers "doing well by doing good", the "win-win" situation of improving relationships while working on good causes. To get our hands around the benefits to the "good cause" requires some additional concepts. Nobel prize-winning economist Amartya Sen has challenged the mainstream growth-focused views of development to focus on development as "a process of expanding the real freedoms that people enjoy"[6] to "lead the lives they have reason to value". Sen argues that development evaluations and policies should focus on what people are able to do and be, on the quality of their life and on removing obstacles in their lives so that they have more freedom to live the kind of life that they have reason to value. Thus, any development

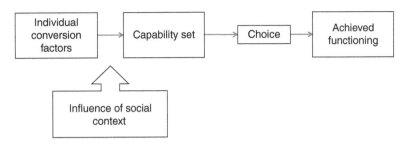

Figure 6.2   The capabilities approach[7]

project should be conceptualized in terms of people's capabilities and their opportunities to undertake the actions and activities they want to engage in. Sen insists that policy makers or evaluators scrutinize the context in which economic production and social interactions take place as the social context influences an individual's capacity to create capabilities (freedom to achieve) from commodities (goods and services). Goods and services are important to the accomplishment of functioning, but this is influenced by "conversion factors", the limitations that might be put on achieving the functioning. Sen identifies three categories of conversion factors: personal (e.g. physical condition, reading skills, intelligence), social (e.g. public policy, social norms, gender norms, social hierarchy, power relations) and environmental (e.g. climate, geographical location).

The approach is summarized in Figure 6.2. The individual conversion factors represent the impact of social context on an individual's ability to convert the means to achieve (such as goods and services) into the freedom to achieve their capabilities. The capabilities approach places great emphasis on these conversion factors and the choices subsequently available to convert capabilities into achievement (functionings).

Reflection on the OSOCOS case

The findings of the Steria–CFS OSOCOS case described in Chapter 4 are briefly summarized in Table 6.1.

The benefits to buyer and provider are strategic as they are clearly large and distinctive. When considering OSOCOS through the capability approach, the computer lab and training represents a commodity. That commodity contributes a capability set for the teachers and children, in particular related to computer literacy. This is important for a developing

Table 6.1 Steria–CFS OSOCOS impacts

Sustainability in global IT outsourcing example	Firm impact	Development impact
Steria and CFS–Steria "One School" program	• Building vendor–client relationships and communications • Workforce benefits • Halo effect	• Two schools received computer center from CFS • Library materials provided by CFS and Steria • Training from vendor

country, as schools are being called on to build the human capital essential for participation in a technologically advanced society that is able to participate in the global economy.[8]

Three management protocols

Viewing the OSOCOS case through the lens of the capability approach presents three key management protocols. These are:

- importance of context;
- limits of the business case for sustainability and
- timescales.

The importance of context

Writing on the case of computers in schools, Hosman[9] argues for a holistic approach. In the author's own words:

> One of the challenges facing many well intentioned ICT-for-education projects is that such projects have traditionally failed to anticipate the importance of such considerations as teacher training, educational outcomes, infrastructural requirements, and the like; in other words, many fail to take a holistic approach to the adoption of the technology. And yet, it is becoming widely recognized that, in order to promote uptake, adoption, and a culture of use (i.e. to achieve sustainable outcomes), a focus that includes the entire ecosystem of a project is necessary. Further challenges include both performing a truthful assessment of the conditions into which ICT is introduced and enumerating realistic goals that the use of ICT is anticipated to achieve.

In order to analyze this "entire ecosystem", Sen posits that availability of goods and services (in this case the computer center and associated training in the Indian school) and realization of functioning (e.g. computer literacy) is influenced by three groups of conversion factors:

- personal (e.g. reading skills, intelligence);
- social (e.g. public policy, social norms, gender norms, social hierarchy, power relations); and
- environmental (e.g. climate, geographical location).

An example where personal conversion factors were given insufficient consideration is shown in Case 6.2.

Case 6.2: Digital equalizer faces problems

The "Digital Equalizer" project is organized by the American Indian Foundation. Here, computer labs and equipment are installed in schools in rural areas of India similar to that of the Steria–CFS-sponsored schools. However, the scheme was unsuccessful because many children in the school cannot speak English, and English instructional downloads from the Internet required translation, which was unavailable.

The social level is illustrated in primary education in India, which is socially complex and multifaceted, containing multiple actors and stakeholders (e.g. social movements, government and non-governmental organizations) with differing, sometimes conflicting, political interests. Sinha[10] points out that the introduction of computers in education involves embedding within existing social and gender relations and their use is subject to asymmetries in power. For instance, in some societies such as Egypt and Saudi Arabia, men and women have considerably different access to the Internet.[11]

An example of the environmental consideration is shown in the often slow or non-existent Internet access or frequent power cuts, which are commonplace in Indian rural areas. Hosman[12] identifies the long-term power costs involved with setting up computer labs in schools as problematic, as electricity in rural areas is often expensive, meaning that the least costly methods for operating computers should be taken into consideration and solar power or other renewable sources of energy should be considered.

Lesson

- Consider the contextual details of the chosen GITO collaborative intervention taking account of personal, social and environmental conversion factors that may help or hinder capability achievement of the target group.

The business case for shared value

Porter and Kramer[13] argue that "the essential test that should guide CSR is not whether a cause is worthy but whether it presents an opportunity to create shared value". Thus, their starting point is business imperatives and not capabilities and achieved functionings. Hosman[14] points out that "despite the promise that today's new technologies hold, the unplanned introduction of ICT – without a realistic understanding of what technology can and cannot do, or of which capabilities it may enhance – can intensify existing inequalities in society and lead to disappointments". In this case, the use of Porter and Kramer's approach to guide the school sponsorship appears to succumb to Tencati and Zsolnai's[15] critique as "an add-on element to the traditional [competitive strategy] framework... CSR is only considered an additional instrument to achieve a better competitive performance".

Porter and Kramer do not prescribe that the "good causes" have any participation in the debate about what capability sets should be introduced. In the OSOCOS case, it is a computer lab in a school. How are we to know if that is the most appropriate capability set for the school over, for example toilets or more teachers? Hosman argues that providing schools with computers without addressing underlying educational issues or attempting to anticipate how their presence would change the learning environment is a "fruitless endeavor". Mooij's study of the teachers' perspective on problems in Indian primary schools does not reveal a priority for introduction of computers.[16]

By contrast, the capability approach encourages the process of participation and public discussion in deciding the capability sets as well as in the resulting change. The approach further requires attention to participation around decisions as to what capabilities are to count in any particular collective or society.

Lesson

Encourage participation of the beneficiaries of the chosen intervention and ensure that their views are fully considered alongside the business case.

Long-term versus short-term sustainability

Our third point of critique is the question of the longer-term bene-fits of the GITO collaborative sustainability. Reflecting on the OSOCOS project, Hosman points out that installing computers in schools is a long-term investment. In addition to teacher training and support (from the government, administrators and parents), there are other important con-siderations that must be part of the investment equation for the developing world. Infrastructure and human capital investment requires upkeep and reinvestment at a much faster pace than do traditional infrastructural cap-ital investments. First, human capital needs to be considered: training and support must be offered on an initial and ongoing basis. Second, equipment will need to be maintained, and hardware and software will need to be updated when they become outdated or obsolete. Furthermore, the Steria employees assigned to the school are volunteers who are fully engaged in employment in a hectic, intense work environment typical of an India-based outsourcing processing center. Thus, the mentoring and training toward the functionings is dependent on the goodwill of vol-unteers, which in a period of heightened workload may be withdrawn. Moreover, there is much evidence that market-based outsourcing is tenta-tive where contracts may be canceled and are subject to renewal. In this case, unless another sponsor could be found, non-renewal would lead to the withdrawal of sponsorship, including any essential software and hardware upgrades that fulfill the associated capability set. Outsourcing contracts, which are typically for a five-year period, are liable to be dis-lodged by a change of management or a swing in the business cycle. For example, on takeover in 2005, the AND 1 shoe company incoming management canceled all social programs.[17]

Lesson

Consider the timescales of the project – is the commitment enough to pro-vide long-term development? Is there a transition plan if the collaboration is canceled?

Incorporating socially responsible outsourcing

A number of researchers have examined the model of socially respon-sible outsourcing or, simply, social outsourcing. This model is built on the concept of outsourcing of work to a disadvantaged group in soci-ety, often with governmental support, with the intention of sustainable improvement of the livelihoods for those providing the service. This area of research has blended a developmental perspective on outsourcing and has paid attention to the long-term implications of sustainability projects. Research projects are described in Cases 6.3 and 6.4, and each provides some perspective on the long-term implications of socially responsible and sustainable outsourcing.

Case 6.3: Kerala State poverty eradication mission

In one examination of social outsourcing, Heeks and Arun undertook a case study of the Kerala State Poverty Eradication Mission in India to understand if social outsourcing could deliver development benefits sought by the government.[18] The program established hundreds of social enterprises that cover a wide range of activities, including clothing production, food processing and information technology outsourcing. All of the social enterprises were operated and staffed by women from poor communities whose average earnings each were US$45 per month. A key outcome from the program was that the social outsourcing scheme had allowed the women to achieve higher incomes and greater income stability. More than half of the enterprises had been running for more than six years, and more than 90% had been running for more than four years. The authors conclude that the initiative demonstrated how social outsourcing can be used to bring direct benefits to members of poor communities in developing countries.

Case 6.4: Rural outsourcing in the United States

Lacity et al. examined the phenomena of rural outsourcing to understand how IT and business process outsourcing services can be delivered from remote domestic locations.[19] They note that remote outsourcing providers rely on untapped populations for both profit and social reasons. For example, in the United States these providers work with Native Americans, blue-collar workers, returning war veterans and even prison labor. They also note that some remote outsourcing providers have a strong social mission, such as Samasource, whose non-profit mission is to provide a living wage for marginalized workers living in the poorest countries. The researchers conclude that rural or remote outsourcing is growing quickly for several reasons such as the desire to keep domestic work onshore, for economic reasons as buyers search for ongoing low-cost, high-quality labor pools and finally for social reasons to provide a living wage for a disadvantaged group. Although the research covered locations in India, Israel, China and the United States, it did not examine the long-term sustainability of this new outsourcing model.

GITO collaborative sustainability and innovation

Willcocks et al.[20] have explored the need for collaboration as a prerequisite for innovation. Their findings and frameworks for trust also apply to collaborative sustainability. They state that innovation in outsourcing requires a higher level of trust to create an opportunity that all parties can benefit from. The authors cite the Heathrow Terminal Five (T5) project as an example of innovative collaboration, noting that "investing in people and in understanding relationships" was one of the key learning points for success of this outsourcing project.

Willcocks et al. identify the need for a flexible contract to encourage and not constrain innovation. In one case study at Spring Global Mail they found that "without trust there can be no innovation" and that "trust is built by letting some things go". Most importantly, they identify a highly structured contract as being counterproductive to creating trust: "once you go back to the contract you are in a fight and trust is lost". Similarly at the T5 project the contract was seen as a structure to encourage the right behavior with integrated teams and integrated team values. As the T5 construction director stated "we did not simply rely on a contract that identifies culpability when something goes wrong".

Willcocks et al. identify creative contracting with leadership, organization and teaming as the fundamental requirements for behavior change to move from a low-trust to a high-trust relationship. They advocate moving from a power-based outsourcing relationship, which is essentially an adversarial game to a high-trust partnership-based relationship.

Figure 6.3 has been adapted from Willcocks et al.[21] to show the behavior changes in moving from a low-trust outsourcing relationship to a high-trust relationship.

In adapting the Willcocks model to our collaborative sustainability model described in this book, the same characteristics are evident. For example, as we found at CFS, trust and communication is built through the intervention developing the partnering behaviors, which Willcocks

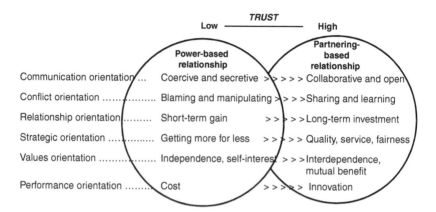

Figure 6.3 Changing from low-trust to high-trust relationship
Source: Willcocks et al. (2011).

argues are key to innovation payoff. In the Steria–CFS case, the OSOCOS project operates outside of the standard outsourcing contract, but it may be possible to include some aspects of sustainability collaboration in a formalized contract within the main contractual agreement or separated with elements such as:

- the shared responsibilities;
- management meetings for reporting; and
- monitoring and controlling, ensuring progression of the project.

Where appropriate, linking the contract to measuring the dimensions of capability achievement of those individuals or groups in the chosen intervention would be desirable.

Conclusion

Writing in 2012, it seems likely that recession would continue with financial crisis in markets and indebted European countries (such as Greece and Ireland). Outsourcing is seen as one important mechanism for saving money. However, the lessons of the past show that managing GITO is a fraught area littered with failure. This book has investigated the role that "doing well by doing good" can play as a means for improving the relationship and productivity between GITO transacting partners. GITO is a remarkable setting because of the growth of the outsourcing sector and the partnering between firms. This chapter has focused on the benefit to the chosen group that constitutes the intervention. The addition of emphasis on development reveals the context, the multitude of stakeholders and limits of the instrumental choices firms may make on the basis of restricted commercially oriented priorities without participation of those affected for consideration of the priorities. All of this leaves us with two main conclusions:

- Doing well by doing good is achievable in the right circumstances between the right partners at the right time. The Steria–CFS OSOCOS case shows that there are "win-win" benefits to be achieved that go some way to facilitating partnership and team building.
- Managers should apply careful, thoughtful reflective planning and genuine attention to the social and environmental causes while being aware of commercial imperatives.

This research has only begun to scratch the surface of sustainability in outsourcing. As we have met with, interviewed, presented to and discussed this topic with global buyers and providers of outsourcing, as well as advisors and other researchers, their level of interest has grown.

Three potential areas of future study are apparent. These are the establishment of a longitudinal study to follow up on the case information presented in this paper; a global study to examine best practices in collaborative sustainability in outsourcing; and a focus on remote or rural sourcing and collaborative sustainability to examine the role of third parties in fostering these types of projects. Each of these areas is discussed below.

First, a longitudinal study that compares the value of sustainability in outsourcing to the buyer, provider and to the society would demonstrate the durability of this concept and show that the case-study results in this research are not temporary. Moreover, revisiting the case studies in this paper would show how the relationship has developed, or not, with collaborative sustainability. Such a longitudinal study should revisit the CFS–Steria case and would be able to track increasing value such as additional schools supported by the collaborative sustainability program. The study would also revisit the strength of the relationship to determine how increased trust has been used to bridge the challenges of the outsourcing relationship and to extend the commercial value of the relationship, a key outcome of which would be the ability of Steria to extend its outsourcing work with CFS. At the same time, the role of an other outsourcing providers and their receptivity to collaborative sustainability with CFS will be an interesting development to examine.

Second, a global outsourcing industry study should compare different collaborative sustainability programs to understand best practices and to determine where the buyers and providers are able to create the greatest and most durable shared value for society. This study would be of value to global outsourcing buyers and providers and could be sponsored by one or more of the professional outsourcing bodies, such as the IAOP, NASSCOM or NOA. The IAOP CSR survey conducted in 2009 was repeated in 2011 with results becoming available later in 2012 and could be a precursor to such an industry-wide study. The Rockefeller Foundation has asked to include questions in the survey to explore socially responsible outsourcing in order to understand the opportunities for impact sourcing.[22]

Third, additional research should focus on a combination of rural sourcing,[23] which is also called impact sourcing, within the context of regular industry-based outsourcing arrangements. This research should examine whether outsourcing providers would take up collaborative sustainability projects such as impact sourcing within a regular business model of their own volition or would third parties (such as governments or NGOs or charitable foundations) be needed to encourage collaborative sustainability.

Notes

Introduction: Achieving social and environmental responsibility in global outsourcing

1. NASSCOM. (2011). "Green IT Initiative: Catalysing Sustainable Environment." Retrieved August 29, 2011, from http://www.nasscom.in/nasscom/templates/LandingNS.aspx?id=55759.
2. International Association of Outsourcing Professionals (IAOP).
3. See Babin, R. and B. Hefley (2010). *Corporate Social Responsibility in Outsourcing: Summary of Findings from the IAOP 2009 CSR Survey*, New York, IAOP: 1–20.
4. The survey question was: "As a customer; when your organization makes outsourcing decisions, have you considered the corporate social responsibility (CSR) capability of the outsourcing provider?"
5. Willcocks, L., S. Cullen, et al. (2011). *The Outsourcing Enterprise. From Cost Management to Collaborative Innovation*. Basingstoke, Palgrave Macmillan.
6. See Lacity and Hirschheim (1993); Sahay, Nicholson, et al. (2003); Dibbern, Goles, et al. (2004); Feeny, Lacity, et al. (2005); Willcocks and Lacity (2006); Oshri, I., J. Kotlarsky, et al. (2009). *The Handbook of Global Outsourcing and Offshoring*. Basingstoke, Palgrave Macmillan; and Lacity, Khan, et al. (2010).
7. Willcocks, L. and M. Lacity (2009). *The Practice of Outsourcing: From ITO to BPO and Offshoring*. London, Palgrave Macmillan: 14.
8. Ibid.
9. NASSCOM (2009). *Outsourcing Industry Trends*. New Delhi, NASSCOM: 1–4.
10. Accenture. (2010c). *Outsourcing 2010: Summary of Findings from IAOP's State of the Industry Survey*. Dublin, Accenture: 1–7: 3.
11. Brundtland, G. H. (1987). *Report of the World Commission on Environment and Development: Our Common Future*. New York, United Nations.
12. Elkington, J. (1994). "Towards the Sustainable Corporation: Win-Win-Win Business Strategies for Sustainable Development." *California Management Review* 36(2): 90–100.
13. Carroll, A. B. (1991). "The Pyramid of Corporate Social Responsibility." *Business Horizons* 34: 39–48.
14. Elkington, J. (1997). *Cannibals with Forks: The Triple Bottom Line of the 21st Century Business*. Oxford, Capstone.
15. Non English titles, and titles using phrases other than CSR or Sustainability, approximately 35% of all the 2010 GRI reports, were excluded from the count.
16. (2010). *Vision 2050: The New Agenda for Business*. Geneva, World Business Council for Sustainable Development: 1–73.
17. Parayil, G. (2005). "The Digital Divide and Increasing Returns: Contradictions of Informational Capitalism." *The Information Society* 21: 41–51.
18. Blinder, A. (2006). "Offshoring: The Next Industrial Revolution?" *Foreign Affairs* 85(2): 113–123.

19. Jones, M. (2005). "The Transnational Corporation, Corporate Social Responsibility and the 'Outsourcing' Debate." *The Journal of American Academy of Business* 6(2): 91–97.

20. Levy, D. (2005). "Offshoring in the New Global Political Economy." *Journal of Management Studies* 42(3): 685–693.

21. Knorringa, P. and L. Pegler (2006). "Globalisation, Firm Upgrading and Impacts on Labour." *Royal Dutch Geographical Society* 97(5): 470–479.

22. DeGeorge, R. (2006). "Information Technology, Globalization and Ethics." *Ethics and Information Technology* 8: 29–40.

23. Stainer, L. and S. Grey (2007). "The Ethical Landscape of Outsourcing Performance." *International Journal of Business Performance Management* 9(4): 453–469.

24. Ibid.

1   Why is Sustainable Outsourcing Important?

1. Goolsby, K. and F. K. Whitlow (2004). *Eight Buyer-Provider Disconnect Areas Likely to Cause Outsourcing Failures.* Dallas, TX, The Outsourcing Center: 1–19.

2. Willcocks, L., S. Cullen, et al. (2011). *The Outsourcing Enterprise. From Cost Management to Collaborative Innovation.* Basingstoke, Hampshire, Palgrave Macmillan.

3. *The Times,* Friday December 9 2011.

4. See for instance Willcocks et al. (2011). *The Outsourcing Enterprise.*

5. Hoek, R. V. and M. Johnson (2010). "Sustainability and Energy Efficiency: Research Implications from an Academic Roundtable and Two Case Examples." *International Journal of Physical Distribution & Logistics Management* 40(1/2): 148–158.

6. The terms onshore, offshore and nearshore are covered in detail in Lacity, M. C. and J. W. Rottman (2008). *Offshore Outsourcing of IT Work: Client and Supplier Perspectives.* Hampshire, Palgrave Macmillan. In short "off-shore" refers to the practice of hiring outsourcing providers in another country, usually distant from the buyer location. For example, UK firms will hire Indian firms to provide software support. When the outsourcing provider is in a nearby location, for example a US buyer outsourcing to Canada, the relationship is usually referred to as "near-shore". For additional definitions, refer to Oshri, I., J. Kotlarsky, et al. (2009). *The Handbook of Global Outsourcing and Offshoring.* Hampshire, Palgrave Macmillan.

7. Greenpeace. (2011). "Cool IT Leaderboard." Retrieved August 29, 2011, from http://www.greenpeace.org/international/en/campaigns/climate-change/cool-it/leaderboard/.

8. Friedman, M. (1970). "The Social Responsibility of Business is to Increase its Profits." *New York Times* (September 13) New York.

9. Pinkston, T. S. and A. B. Carroll (1996). "A Retrospective Examination of CSR Orientations: Have They Changed?" *Journal of Business Ethics* 15(2): 199.

10. Carroll, A. (1991). "The Pyramid of Corporate Social Responsibility: Toward the Moral Management of Organizational Stakeholders." *Business Horizons* 34: 39–48.

11. For a discussion on the need to balance the syndrome of organizational self-ishness with social responsibility and cooperative human engagement see Mintzberg, H., R. Simons, et al. (2002). "Beyond Selfishness." *Sloan Management Review* **Fall:** 67–74; and Rendtorff, J. D. (2009). *Responsibility, Ethics and Legitimacy of Corporations*. Frederiksberg, Copenhagen Business School Press.

12. Falck, O. and S. Heblich (2007). "Corporate Social Responsibility: Doing Well by Doing Good." *Business Horizons* 50: 247–254.

13. See Emerson, J. (2003). "The Blended Value Proposition: Integrating Social and Financial Returns." *California Management Review* **45**(4): 35–51; and Elkington, J., J. Emerson, et al. (2006). "The Value Palette: A Tool for full Spectrum Strategy." *California Management Review* **48**(2): 6–28.

14. See Porter, M. E. and M. R. Kramer (2006). "Strategy and Society: The Link between Competitive Advantage and Corporate Social Responsibility." *Harvard Business Review* **84**(12): 78–92; Falck and Heblich (2007) "Corporate Social Responsibility"; Vilanova, M., J. M. Lozano, et al. (2009). "Exploring the Nature of the Relationship between CSR and Competitiveness." *Journal of Business Ethics* **87**: 57–69; and Porter, M. E. and M. R. Kramer (2011). "Creating Shared Value." *Harvard Business Review* **89**(1/2): 63–77.

15. Samasource CEO Leila Chirayath Janah, Janah, L. C. (2009). *Socially Responsible Outsourcing: Promoting Equal Access to Opportunities in Low-Income Regions*. The 2009 Asia-Pacific Outsourcing Summit, Kuala Lumpur.

16. Heeks, R. and S. Arun (2009). "Social Outsourcing as a Development Tool: The Impact of Outsourcing IT Services to Women's Social Enterprises in Kerala." *Journal of International Development* 22: 441–454.

17. Lacity, M., J. Rottman, et al. (2010). "Field of Dreams: Building IT Capabilities in Rural America." *Strategic Outsourcing International Journal* 3(3): 169–191.

18. Nyoro, J. (2011). *Job Creation through Building the Field of Impact Sourcing*. New York, Rockefeller Foundation: 1–40.

19. Nidumolu, R., C. K. Prahalad, et al. (2009). "Why Sustainability Is Now the Key Driver of Innovation." *Harvard Business Review* **87**(9): 56–64.

20. See Carmel and Tija (2005), for example, who identify that global outsourcing incurs management costs and in most cases there is an increase in global flights of staff (e.g. from India) back and forth to client sites in the United Kingdom, for example.

21. Lewis, N. S. (2007). "Powering the Planet." *Material Research Society (MRS) Bulletin* 32(October): 808–820.

22. Koomey, J. G. (2008). "Worldwide Electricity Used in Data Centers." *Environmental Research Letters* 3: 8.

23. Koomey, J. G. (2011). *Growth in Data Center Electricity Use 2005 to 2010*. Palo Alto, CA, Stanford University: 20.

24. Laitner, J. and K. Ehrhardt-Martinez (2008). *Information and Communications Technologies: The Power of Productivity – How ICT Sectors Are Driving Gains in Energy Productivity*. Washington, DC, American Council for an Energy Efficient Economy.

25. Ibid., p. 9.

26. (2008). *Code of Conduct on Data Centres Energy Efficiency Version 1.0*. Ispra, European Commission – Institute for Energy, Renewable Energies Unit: 1–20.

27. NOA (2009). *Greensourcing: The Challenges Facing the Business World*. London, National Outsourcing Association – Green Steering Committee: 1–11.

28. Mason, K. (2008). *A Carbon Reduction Framework for Buyers of Business Travel*. Cranfield, Business Travel Research Centre, Cranfield University: 1–54.

29. Jackson, R. B., S. R. Carpenter, et al. (2001). "Water in a Changing World." *Ecological Applications* **11**(4): 1027–1045.

30. Crane, A., D. Matten, et al. (2008). *Corporate Social Responsibility, Readings and Cases in Global Context*, London, Routledge.

31. For example, Willis, A. (2003). "The Role of the Global Reporting Initiative's Sustainability Reporting Guidelines in the Social Screening of Investments." *Journal of Business Ethics* **43**(3): 233–237.

32. GRI. (2011). "What is GRI?" Retrieved March 11, 2012, from https://www.globalreporting.org/information/about-gri/Pages/default.aspx.

33. UN. (2008). "Overview of the UN Global Compact." Retrieved December 3, 2008, from www.unglobalcompact.org/aboutthegc.

34. UN. (2010). "UN Global Compact and Global Reporting Initiative Announce New Collaboration." Retrieved August 29, 2011, from https://www.global reporting.org/information/about-gri/alliances-and-synergies/Pages/United-Nations-Global-Compact.aspx.

35. For a discussion of Nike's role in creating labour standards in developing countries, see Zadak, S. (2004). "The Path to Corporate Responsibility." *Harvard Business Review* **82**(12): 125–132; and Klein, N. (2000). *No Logo*. Toronto, ON, Vintage.

36. For a discussion on the role of CSR in protecting the corporate brand, see Werther, W. B. and D. Chandler (2005). "Strategic Corporate Social Responsibility as Global Brand Insurance." *Business Horizons* **48**: 317–324; and Falck and Heblich (2007). "Corporate Social Responsibility": 247–254.

37. Bhattacharya, C. B., S. Sen, et al. (2008). "Using Corporate Social Responsibility to Win the War for Talent." *MIT Sloan Management Review* **49**(2): 37–44

38. Foster, (2009) *The Green IT Review*. Retrieved May 30, 2009, from www.thegreenitreview.com.

39. PriceWaterhouseCoopers. (2009). Carbon Disclosure Project 2009, Global 500 Report.

40. Flanagan, R. (2011). "Australia's Carbon Tax is a Brave Start by a Government Still Griped by Fear." *The Guardian*. Retrieved August 29, 2011, from http://www.guardian.co.uk/commentisfree/2011/jul/10/australia-carbon-tax-modest-beginning.

41. The CORE survey data was collected during 2008 and 2009 during outsourcing education classes. IAOP agreed to conduct a similar electronic survey of its members in 2009. The results of the survey were presented at the IAOP February 2010 Outsourcing Summit. NOA conducted a similar survey, again with six questions that were aligned with both the CORE and IAOP surveys. The survey was distributed electronically to NOA members, and the results were collected in March/April 2010.

42. For a discussion of rural sourcing in the United States, see Lacity et al. (2010). "Field of dreams": 169–191. For a global discussion about remote outsourcing, see Lacity, M., E. Carmel, et al. (2011). "Rural Outsourcing: Delivering ITO and BPO Services from Remote Domestic Locations." *Computer* **44**(12): 55–62.

2   Integrating Sustainability and Outsourcing

1. Enbridge (2011). *Enbridge Inc. 2010 Annual Report.* p. 36.
2. Nunn, S. (2007). *Green IT: Beyond the Data Center. How It Can Contribute to the Environmental Agenda across and beyond the Business.* Dublin, Accenture: 1–8.
3. Accenture (2010a). *Cloud Computing and Sustainability: The Environmental Benefits of Moving to the Cloud.* Dublin, Accenture: 1–14.
4. Rio Tinto. (2009). "The Way We Work: Our Global Code of Business Conduct." Retrieved August 29, 2011, from http://www.procurement.riotinto.com/ENG/supplierregistration/34_the_way_we_work.asp.
5. Rio Tinto. (2006). "The Way We Buy: Our Statement of Procurement Practice." Retrieved August 29, 2011, from http://www.procurement.riotinto.com/ENG/supplierregistration/34_the_way_we_buy.asp.

3   Measuring Sustainability

1. We used the IAOP 2008 list of top outsourcing providers to identify a list of 19 leading GITO providers. We then examined the GITO providers' website to assess whether they participated in any of the global sustainability standards. The IAOP Global Outsourcing 100 provides a representative set GITO organizations as a proxy representing the GITO provider market. The list of leading GITO outsourcers was refined in two ways. First, the research focused on the top 25 outsourcers to understand if sustainability patterns could be determined that would be applicable to the remaining 75 organizations. Second, we focused on GITO providers, removing non-IT industries such as food service and real estate service. This resulted in a list of 19 GITO providers.

   We focused on four global sustainability standards (GRI, CDP, ISO 26000/14001 and UN Global Compact) that represent sustainability capability. In addition, we looked at SRI indices such as the DJSI, the FTSE-4-Good Index and the Standard and Poor Environmental Social and Corporate Governance (S&P ESG) Index, which suggest that a publically traded outsource provider is considered as a Socially Responsible Investment. We then examined the provider website for any mention of the sustainability criteria established above. When a sustainability criterion was mentioned the provider reference was cross-checked with the standards organization of the auditing organization for verification (e.g. GRI, CDP, ISO, UN). Undoubtedly, the results presented here will change, likely with growing sustainability participation, as organizations update their websites over time to reflect increased sustainability capability.
2. Examples of stages of growth and maturity models can be found in Holland and Light (2001); Carmel and Agarwal (2002); and Gottschalk and Solli-Saether (2006).
3. See Nolan, R. (1973). "Managing the Computer Resource: A Stage Hypothesis." *Communications of the ACM* 16(7): 399–405, and Nolan, R. (1974). "Managing the Four Stages of EDP Growth." *Harvard Business Review* 52(1) and finally, Nolan, R. (1979). "Managing the Crisis in Data Processing." *Harvard Business Review* 57(2).
4. Galliers and Sutherland reviewed the stages-of-growth models from different authors, citing the Nolan model as the "seminal influence" and "one of the 15

most cited by information systems researchers". They propose a more broadly focused model "incorporating strategic, organizational, human resource and management considerations". The authors define a six-stage model that is more robust than do Nolan's, moving from "Ad-hocracy" (stage 1) to Integrated harmonious relationships (stage 6). The purpose of these models is to outline how organizations should move from early stages of development to more mature stages, while laying appropriate groundwork to better ensure success at later stages. This is also how our sustainability stages-of-growth model should be used.

5. Nidumolu, R., C. K. Prahalad, et al. (2009). "Why Sustainability is Now the Key Driver of Innovation." *Harvard Business Review* **87**(9): 56–64.
6. CSC. (2011). "About Us: Our Purpose is Clear." Retrieved August 29, 2011, from http://www.csc.com/about_us.
7. Carmel, E. and B. Nicholson (2005). "Small Firms and Offshore Software Outsourcing: High Transaction Costs and Their Mitigation." *Journal of Global Information Management* **13**(3): 33–54.
8. Porter, M. and M. Kramer (1999). "Philanthropy's New Agenda: Creating Value." *Harvard Business Review* **77**(6): 121–130. Porter, M. and M. Kramer (2002). "The Competitive Advantage of Corporate Philanthropy." *Harvard Business Review* **80**(12): 57–68. Porter, M. and M. Kramer (2006). "Strategy and Society: The Link Between Competitive Advantage and Corporate Social Responsibility." *Harvard Business Review* **84**(12): 78–92. Porter, M. and M. Kramer (2011). "Creating Shared Value." *Harvard Business Review* **89**(1/2): 63–77.
9. Friedman, M. (1970). "The Social Responsibility of Business is to Increase its Profits." *New York Times* (September 13) New York.
10. Franklin, D. (2008). Just Good for Business. *The Economist* (January 19): 1–24.
11. NASSCOM, D. (2008). *Indian IT/ITES Industry: Impacting Economy and Society 2007-2008*. New Delhi, NASSCOM Foundation: 1–79.
12. Lowitt, E. M., A. J. Hoffman, et al. (2009). *Sustainability and Its Impact on the Corporate Agenda*. Dublin, Accenture: 1–31.
13. Accenture (2010b). *A New Era of Sustainability*. Dublin, Accenture.
14. Nunn, S. (2007). *Green IT: Beyond the Data Center. How IT Can Contribute to the Environmental Agenda across and beyond the Business*, Dublin, Accenture: 1–8.
15. (2010). *Vision 2050: The New Agenda for Business*. Geneva, World Business Council for Sustainable Development: 1–73.
16. Porter and Kramer (2006). "Strategy and Society".
17. Trust in business relationships has been examined by several researchers: Lewicki, R. J. and B. B. Bunker (1996). "Developing and Maintaining Trust in Work Relationships (Chapter 7)". *Trust in Organizations, Frontiers of Theory and Research*. R. M. Kramer and T. R. Tyler, Thousand Oaks, CA, Sage: 114–139; Sabherwal (1999). "The Role of Trust in Outsourced IS Development Projects." *Communications of the ACM* **42**(2): 80–86; Heiskanen, A., M. Newman, et al. (2008). "Control, Trust, Power, and the Dynamics of Information Systems Outsourcing Relationships: A Process Study of Contractual Software Development." *Journal of Strategic Information Systems* **17**: 268–286.
18. Brokaw (2009). "Does Sustainability Change the Talent Equation." *MIT Sloan Management Review* **51**(1): 33–34.

19. Werther, W. B. and D. Chandler (2005). "Strategic Corporate Social Responsibility as Global Brand Insurance." *Business Horizons* **48**: 317–324.
20. Lewis, N. S. (2007). "Powering the Planet." *Material Research Society (MRS) Bulletin* **32**(October): 808–820.
21. EPA (2007). *Report to Congress on Server and Data Center Energy Efficiency.* Washington, DC, US Environmental Protection Agency.
22. Koomey, J. G. (2011). *Growth in Data Center Electricity Use 2005 to 2010.* Palo Alto, CA, Stanford University: 20.
23. Brown-Wilson, G. (2009). *Green Outsourcing Survey.* Clearwater, FL, Wilson: 3.
24. Nethope. (2011). "Nethope: Wiring the Global Village." Retrieved August 29, 2011, from http://www.nethope.org/about/us/.

4 Collaborating for Shared Value

1. Porter, M. E. and M. R. Kramer (2006). "Strategy and Society: The Link Between Competitive Advantage and Corporate Social Responsibility." *Harvard Business Review* **84**(12): 92.
2. Kern and Willcocks (2000) Op cit
3. For a discussion on trust, see Lewicki, R. J. and B. B. Bunker (1996). "Developing and Maintaining Trust in Work Relationships (Chapter 7)." *Trust in Organizations, Frontiers of Theory and Research.* R. M. Kramer and T. R. Tyler, Thousand Oaks, CA, Sage: 114–139.
4. Fairbairn, B. (1994). *The Meaning of Rochdale. Regina, Canada, Centre for the Study of Co-operatives.* Saskatchewan, University of Saskatchewan: 5.
5. The Co-operative Group. (2011). *Building a Better Society: Annual Report and Accounts 2010.* Manchester, The Co-operative Group: 1–180.
6. Steria. (2011). *Registration Document 2010.* Paris, Group Steria SCA: 1–232.
7. See for example Oza, N. V., T. Hall, et al. (2006). "Trust in Software Outsourcing Relationships: An Empirical Investigation of Indian Software Companies." *Information and Software Technology* **48**: 345–354; Sabherwal (1999). "The Role of Trust in Outsourced IS Development Projects." *Communications of the ACM* **42**(2): 80–86.
8. Porter and Kramer (2006). "Strategy and Society": 88.
9. Ibid.: 90.
10. Lewicki and Bunker (1996). "Developing and Maintaining Trust in Work Relationships (Chapter 7)."
11. Ibid.: 119.
12. Ibid.: 121.
13. Sabherwal (1999). "The Role of Trust in Outsourced IS Development Projects.": 81.
14. Scheiber, N. (2004). "As a Center for Outsourcing, India Could Be Losing Its Edge." *New York Times.* New York.
15. Bowman, T. J. (2004). *Spirituality at Work: An Exploratory Sociological Investigation of the Ford Motor Company.* London, The London School of Economics and Political Science. PhD: 340.
16. Amble, B. (2007). "Social responsibility boosts employee engagement." Retrieved August 29, 2011, from http://www.management-issues.com/2007/5/9/research/social-responsibility-boosts-employee-engagement.asp.

17. Berns, M., A. Townend, et al. (2009). "Sustainability and Competitive Advantage." *MIT Sloan Management Review* **51**(1): 19–26.
18. For example, Parayil, G. (2005). "The Digital Divide and Increasing Returns: Contradictions of Informational Capitalism." *The Information Society* **21**: 41–51; Jones, M. (2005). "The Transnational Corporation, Corporate Social Responsibility and the 'Outsourcing' Debate'." *The Journal of American Academy of Business* **6**(2): 91–97. Levy, D. (2005). "Offshoring in the New Global Political Economy." *Journal of Management Studies* **42**(3): 685–693.
19. Porter, M. E. and M. R. Kramer (2011). "Creating Shared Value." *Harvard Business Review* **89**(1/2): 63–77.

5   Leveraging Sustainability in Relationships

1. See for instance Willcocks, L., S. Cullen, et al. (2011). *The Outsourcing Enterprise. From Cost Management to Collaborative Innovation.* Hampshire, Palgrave Macmillan.
2. Nyoro, J. (2011). *Job Creation through Building the Field of Impact Sourcing.* New York, Rockefeller Foundation: 1–40.
3. Porter, M. E. and M. R. Kramer (2011). "Creating Shared Value." *Harvard Business Review* **89**(1/2): 63–77.
4. Ibid.: 68.
5. As described on the Northern Trust website, www.northerntrust.com, accessed January 12, 2012.

6   Steering a Course on Sustainability

1. See Bies, R. J., J. M. Bartunek, et al. (2007). "Corporations as Social Change Agents: Individual, Interpersonal, Institutional, and Environmental Dynamics." *The Academy of Management Review* **32**(3): 788–793. Also see Edwards, M (2008) *Just Another Emperor? The Myths and Realities of Philanthrocapitalism.* London, Demos, http://archive.demos.org/pub1574.cfm.
2. Michael, B. (2003). "Corporate Social Responsibility in International Development: An Overview and Critique." *Corporate Social Responsibility and Environmental Management* **10**(3): 115–128.
3. Raelin, J. A. (2001). "Public Reflection as the Basis of Learning." *Management Learning* **32**(1): 11–30.
4. Schön, D. A. (1983). *The Reflective Practitioner.* Jackson, TN, Basic Books: 163.
5. Bell, S. and S. Morse (2005). "Delivering Sustainability Therapy in Sustainable Development Projects." *Journal of Environmental Management*, 75(1), 37–51.
6. Sen, A. (1999). *Development as Freedom.* New York, Knopf: 3.
7. Robeyns, I. (2005). "The Capability Approach: a theoretical survey." *Journal of Human Development* **6**(1): 93–117.
8. For a discussion and case study of IT philanthropy in developing countries, see Hosman, L. (2010) "Policy Considerations from a Nationwide IT-in-Education Initiative: Macedonia Connects." *Journal of Information Technology & Politics* **7**(4): 369–383.

9. Ibid.
10. Sinha, C. (2009). "Effects of Education and ICT Use on Gender Relations in Bhutan." *Information Technologies and International Development* 5(3): 21–34.
11. Badran, M. F. (2011). Is ICT empowering women in Egypt? An empirical study. *IFIP WG 9.4*. Katmandu, Nepal. Retrieved August 29, 2011, from http://mak.ac.ug/documents/IFIP/EMPOWERINGWOMENINEGYPT.pdf
12. Ibid.
13. Porter, M. E. and M. R. Kramer (2006). "Strategy and Society: The Link Between Competitive Advantage and Corporate Social Responsibility." *Harvard Business Review* 84(12): 78–92.
14. Hosman. "Policy Considerations."
15. Tencati, A. and L. Zsolnai (2009). "The Collaborative Enterprise." *Journal of Business Ethics* 85: 367–376.
16. Mooij, J. (2008). "Primary Education, Teachers' Professionalism and Social Class about Motivation and Demotivation of Government School Teachers in India." *International Journal of Educational Development* 28(5): 508–523.
17. Edwards (2008). *Just Another Emperor?*.
18. Heeks, R. and S. Arun (2010). "Social Outsourcing as a Development Tool: The Impact of Outsourcing IT Services to Women's Social Enterprises in Kerala." *Journal of International Development* 22: 441–454.
19. Lacity, M., Carmel, E., Rottman, J. (2011). "Rural Outsourcing: Delivering ITO and BPO Services from Remote Domestic Locations." *Computer* 44(12): 55–62.
20. Willcocks, L., S. Cullen, et al. (2011). *The Outsourcing Enterprise. From Cost Management to Collaborative Innovation*. Hampshire, Palgrave Macmillan.
21. Ibid., figure 5.9, p. 155.
22. Nyoro, J. (2011). *Job Creation through Building the Field of Impact Sourcing*. New York, Rockefeller Foundation: 1–40.
23. Lacity, M., J. Rottman, et al. (2010). "Field of Dreams: Building IT Capabilities in Rural America." *Strategic Outsourcing International Journal* 3(3): 169–191; Lacity et al. (2011). "Rural Outsourcing": 55–62.

References

(2008). *Code of Conduct on Data Centres Energy Efficiency Version 1.0*. Ispra, Italy, European Commission, Institute for Energy, Renewable Energies Unit: 1–20.

(2010). *Vision 2050: The New Agenda for Business*. Geneva, World Business Council for Sustainable Development: 1–73.

Accenture. (2010a). *Cloud Computing and Sustainability: The Environmental Benefits of Moving to the Cloud*. Dublin, Accenture: 1–14.

Accenture. (2010b). *A New Era of Sustainability*. Dublin, Accenture.

Accenture. (2010c). *Outsourcing 2010: Summary of Findings from IAOP's State of the Industry Survey*. Dublin, Accenture: 1–7.

Amble, B. (2007). "Social responsibility boosts employee engagement." Retrieved August 29, 2011, from http://www.management-issues.com/2007/5/9/research/social-responsibility-boosts-employee-engagement.asp.

Babin, R. and B. Hefley (2010). *Corporate Social Responsibility in Outsourcing: Summary of Findings from the IAOP 2009 CSR Survey*, New York, IAOP: 1–20.

Babin, R. and B. Nicholson (2009). "Corporate Social and Environmental Responsibility in Global IT Outsourcing." *MIS Quarterly Executive* 8(4): 123–132.

Babin, R. and B. Nicholson (2011). "How Green Is My Outsourcer: Measuring Sustainability in Global IT Outsourcing." *Strategic Outsourcing International Journal* 4(1): 47–66.

Badran, M. F. (2011). "Is ICT empowering women in Egypt? An empirical study." *IFIP WG 9.4*. Katmandu, Nepal.

Bell, S. and S. Morse (2005). "Delivering Sustainability Therapy in Sustainable Development Projects." *Journal of Environmental Management* 75(1): 37–51.

Berns, M., A. Townend, et al. (2009). "Sustainability and Competitive Advantage." *MIT Sloan Management Review* 51(1): 19–26.

Bhattacharya, C. B., D. Korschun, et al. (2009). "Strengthening Stakeholder-Company Relationships Through Mutually Beneficial Corporate Social Responsibility Initiatives." *Journal of Business Ethics* 85: 257–272.

Bies, R. J., J. M. Bartunek, et al. (2007). "Corporations as Social Change Agents: Individual, Interpersonal, Institutional, and Environmental Dynamics." *The Academy of Management Review* 32(3): 788–793.

Blinder, A. (2006). "Offshoring: The Next Industrial Revolution?" *Foreign Affairs* 85(2): 113–123.

Bowman, T. J. (2004). "Spirituality at Work: An Exploratory Sociological Investigation of the Ford Motor Company." London, The London School of Economics and Political Science. PhD: 340.

Brokaw. (2009). "Does Sustainability Change the Talent Equation." *MIT Sloan Management Review* 51(1): 33–34.

Brown-Wilson Group. (2009). *Green Outsourcing Survey*. Clearwater, FL, Brown-Wilson Group.

Brundtland, G. H. (1987). *Report of the World Commission on Environment and Development: Our Common Future*. New York, United Nations.

Carmel, E. and R. Agarwal (2002). "The Maturation of Offshore Sourcing of Information Technology Work." *MIS Quarterly Executive* **1**(2): 65–76.

Carmel, E. and B. Nicholson (2005). "Small Firms and Offshore Software Outsourcing: High Transaction Costs and Their Mitigation." *Journal of Global Information Management* **13**(3): 33–54.

Carmel, E. and P. Tija (2005). *Offshoring Information Technology: Sourcing and Outsourcing to a Global Workforce*, Cambridge University Press.

Carroll, A. B. (1991). "The Pyramid of Corporate Social Responsibility: Toward the Moral Management of Organizational Stakeholders." *Business Horizons* **34**: 39–48.

CGI. (2011). "Corporate Social Responsibility: Contributing to the development of our communities." Retrieved August 29, 2011, from http://www.cgi.com/en/corporate-social-responsibility.

CSC. (2011). "About Us: Our Purpose is Clear." Retrieved August 29, 2011, from http://www.csc.com/about_us.

DeGeorge, R. (2006). "Information Technology, Globalization and Ethics." *Ethics and Information Technology* **8**: 29–40.

Dibbern, J., T. Goles, et al. (2004). "Information Systems Outsourcing: A Survey and Analysis of the Literature." *Data Base for Advancement in Information Systems* **35**(4): 6–102.

Edwards, M. (2008). *Just Another Emperor? The Myths and Realities of Philanthrocapitalism*. London, Demos.

Elkington, J. (1994). "Towards the Sustainable Corporation: Win-Win-Win Business Strategies for Sustainable Development." *California Management Review* **36**(2): 90–100.

Elkington, J. (1997). *Cannibals with Forks: The Triple Bottom Line of the 21st Century Business*. Oxford, Capstone.

Elkington, J., J. Emerson, et al. (2006). "The Value Palette: A Tool for full Spectrum Strategy." *California Management Review* **48**(2): 6–28.

Emerson, J. (2003). "The Blended Value Proposition: Integrating Social and Financial Returns." *California Management Review* **45**(4): 35–51.

Enbridge. (2011). *Enbridge Inc. 2010 Annual Report*. Calgary, AL, Enbridge: 36.

EPA. (2007). *Report to Congress on Server and Data Center Energy Efficiency*. Washington, DC, US Environmental Protection Agency.

Fairbairn, B. (1994). *The Meaning of Rochdale*. Regina, Canada, Centre for the Study of Co-operatives, University of Saskatchewan: 1–53.

Falck, O. and S. Heblich (2007). "Corporate Social Responsibility: Doing Well by Doing Good." *Business Horizons* **50**: 247–254.

Feeny, D., M. Lacity, et al. (2005). "Taking the Measure of Outsourcing Providers." *Sloan Management Review* **46**(3): 42–48.

Flanagan, R. (2011). "Australia's Carbon Tax Is a Brave Start by a Government Still Griped by Fear." *The Guardian*. Retrieved August 29, 2011, from http://www.guardian.co.uk/commentisfree/2011/jul/10/australia-carbon-tax-modest-beginning.

Foster, P. (2009, May 27, 2009). "The impact of carbon legislation on data centres/IT services." *The Green IT Review*. Retrieved May 30, 2009, from http://www.thegreenitreview.com/2009/05/impact-of-carbon-legislation-on-data.html.

Franklin, D. (2008). "Just Good for Business." *The Economist* (January 19): 1–24.

Friedman, M. (1970). "The Social Responsibility of Business Is to Increase Its Profits." *New York Times* (September 13). New York.

Goolsby, K. and F. K. Whitlow (2004). *Eight Buyer-Provider Disconnect Areas Likely to Cause Outsourcing Failures*. Dallas, TX, The Outsourcing Center: 1–19.

Gottschalk, P. and H. Solli-Saether (2006). "Maturity Model for IT Outsourcing Relationships." *Industrial Management & Data Systems* **106**(2): 200–212.

Greenpeace. (2011). "Cool IT Leaderboard." Retrieved August 29, 2011, from http://www.greenpeace.org/international/en/campaigns/climate-change/cool-it/leaderboard/.

GRI. (2011). "What is GRI?" Retrieved August 29, 2011, from http://www.globalreporting.org/AboutGRI/WhatIsGRI/.

Heeks, R. and S. Arun (2009). "Social Outsourcing as a Development Tool: The Impact of Outsourcing IT Services to Women's Social Enterprises in Kerala." *Journal of International Development* **22**: 441–454.

Heeks, R. and S. Arun (2010). "Social Outsourcing as a Development Tool: The Impact of Outsourcing IT Services to Women's Social Enterprises in Kerala." *Journal of International Development* **22**: 441–454.

Heiskanen, A., M. Newman, et al. (2008). "Control, Trust, Power, and the Dynamics of Information Systems Outsourcing Relationships: A Process Study of Contractual Software Development." *Journal of Strategic Information Systems* **17**: 268–286.

Hoek, R. V. and M. Johnson (2010). "Sustainability and Energy Efficiency: Research Implications from an Academic Roundtable and Two Case Examples." *International Journal of Physical Distribution & Logistics Management* **40**(1/2): 148–158.

Holland, C. P. and B. Light (2001). "A stage maturity model for enterprise resource planning systems use." *SIGMIS Database* **32**(2): 34–45.

Hosman, L. "Policy Considerations from a Nationwide IT-in-Education Initiative: Macedonia Connects." *Journal of Information Technology & Politics* **7**(4): 369–383.

Infosys. (2009). *Sustainability Report 2008–2009*. Bangalore, Infosys.

Infosys. (2010). *Sustainability Report 2009–2010*. Bangalore, Infosys.

Jackson, R. B., S. R. Carpenter, et al. (2001). "Water in a Changing World." *Ecological Applications* **11**(4): 1027–1045.

Janah, L. C. (2009). *Socially Responsible Outsourcing: Promoting Equal Access to Opportunities in Low-Income Regions*. The 2009 Asia-Pacific Outsourcing Summit, Kuala Lumpur.

Jones, M. (2005). "The Transnational Corporation, Corporate Social Responsibility and the 'Outsourcing' Debate." *The Journal of American Academy of Business* **6**(2): 91–97.

Kern, T. and L. Willcocks (2000). "Exploring information technology outsourcing relationships: theory and practice." *Journal of Strategic Information Systems* **9**: 321–350.

Klein, N. (2000). *No Logo*. Toronto, ON, Vintage.

Knorringa, P. and L. Pegler (2006). "Globalisation, Firm Upgrading and Impacts on Labour." *Royal Dutch Geographical Society* **97**(5): 470–479.

Koomey, J. G. (2008). "Worldwide Electricity Used in Data Centers." *Environmental Research Letters* **3**: 8.

Koomey, J. G. (2011). *Growth in Data Center Electricity Use 2005 to 2010*. Palo Alto, CA, Stanford University: 20.

Lacity, M., E. Carmel, et al. (2011). "Rural Outsourcing: Delivering ITO and BPO Services from Remote Domestic Locations." *Computer* **44**(12): 55–62.

Lacity, M., J. Rottman, et al. (2010). "Field of Dreams: Building IT Capabilities in Rural America." *Strategic Outsourcing International Journal* **3**(3): 169–191.

Lacity, M., S. Khan, et al. (2010). "A review of the IT outsourcing empirical literature and future research directions." *Journal of Information Technology* **25**: 395–433.

Lacity, M. C. and R. Hirschheim (1993). *Information Systems Outsourcing: Myths, Metaphors and Realities*, John Wiley & Sons.

Lacity, M. C. and J. W. Rottman (2008). *Offshore Outsourcing of IT Work: Client and Supplier Perspectives*. Hampshire, Palgrave Macmillan.

Laitner, J. and K. Ehrhardt-Martinez (2008). *Information and Communications Technologies: The Power of Productivity – How ICT Sectors Are Driving Gains in Energy Productivity*. Washington, DC, American Council for an Energy Efficient Economy.

Levy, D. (2005). "Offshoring in the New Global Political Economy." *Journal of Management Studies* **42**(3): 685–693.

Lewicki, R. J. and B. B. Bunker (1996). "Developing and Maintaining Trust in Work Relationships (Chapter 7)." *Trust in Organizations, Frontiers of Theory and Research*. R. M. Kramer and T. R. Tyler, Thousand Oaks, CA, Sage: 114–139.

Lewis, N. S. (2007). "Powering the Planet." *Material Research Society (MRS) Bulletin* **32**(October): 808–820.

Lowitt, E. M., A. J. Hoffman, et al. (2009). *Sustainability and Its Impact on the Corporate Agenda*. Dublin, Accenture: 1–31.

Mason, K. (2008). *A Carbon Reduction Framework for Buyers of Business Travel*. Cranfield, Business Travel Research Centre, Cranfield University: 1–54.

Michael, B. (2003). "Corporate Social Responsibility in International Development: An Overview and Critique." *Corporate Social Responsibility and Environmental Management* **10**(3): 115–128.

Mintzberg, H., R. Simons, et al. (2002). "Beyond Selfishness." *Sloan Management Review* **Fall**: 67–74.

Mooij, J. (2008). "Primary Education, Teachers' Professionalism and Social Class about Motivation and Demotivation of Government School Teachers in India." *International Journal of Educational Development* **28**(5): 508–523.

NASSCOM, D. (2008). *Indian IT/ITES Industry: Impacting Economy and Society 2007–2008*. New Delhi, NASSCOM Foundation: 1–79.

NASSCOM. (2009). *Outsourcing Industry Trends*. New Delhi, NASSCOM: 1–4.

NASSCOM. (2011). "Green IT Initiative: Catalysing Sustainable Environment." Retrieved August 29, 2011, from http://www.nasscom.in/nasscom/templates/LandingNS.aspx?id=55759.

Nethope. (2011). "Nethope: Wiring the Global Village." Retrieved August 29, 2011, from http://www.nethope.org/about/us/.

Nidumolu, R., C. K. Prahalad, et al. (2009). "Why Sustainability is Now the Key Driver of Innovation." *Harvard Business Review* **87**(9): 56–64.

NOA. (2009). *Greensourcing: The Challenges Facing the Business World*. London, National Outsourcing Association, Green Steering Committee: 1–11.

Nolan, R. (1973). "Managing the Computer Resource: A Stage Hypothesis." *Communications of the ACM* **16**(7): 399–405.

Nunn, S. (2007). *Green IT: Beyond the Data Center. How IT Can Contribute to the Environmental Agenda across and beyond the Business.* Dublin, Accenture: 1–8.

Nyoro, J. (2011). *Job Creation through Building the Field of Impact Sourcing.* New York, Rockefeller Foundation: 1–40.

Oshri, I., J. Kotlarsky, et al. (2009). *The Handbook of Global Outsourcing and Offshoring.* Hampshire, Palgrave Macmillan.

Oza, N. V., T. Hall, et al. (2006). "Trust in software outsourcing relationships: An empirical investigation of Indian software companies." *Information and Software Technology* **48**: 345–354.

Parayil, G. (2005). "The Digital Divide and Increasing Returns: Contradictions of Informational Capitalism." *The Information Society* **21**: 41–51.

Pinkston, T. S. and A. B. Carroll (1996). "A Retrospective Examination of CSR Orientations: Have They Changed?" *Journal of Business Ethics* **15**(2): 199.

Porter, M. and M. Kramer (1999). "Philanthropy's New Agenda: Creating Value." *Harvard Business Review* **77**(6): 121–130.

Porter, M. and M. Kramer (2002). "The Competitive Advantage of Corporate Philanthropy." *Harvard Business Review* **80**(12): 57–68.

Porter, M. E. and M. R. Kramer (2006). "Strategy and Society: The Link Between Competitive Advantage and Corporate Social Responsibility." *Harvard Business Review* **84**(12): 78–92.

Porter, M. E. and M. R. Kramer (2011). "Creating Shared Value." *Harvard Business Review* **89**(1/2): 63–77.

PriceWaterhouseCoopers. (2009). *Carbon Disclosure Project 2009, Global 500 Report.*

Raelin, J. A. (2001). "Public Reflection as the Basis of Learning." *Management Learning* **32**(1): 11–30.

Rendtorff, J. D. (2009). *Responsibility, Ethics and Legitimacy of Corporations.* Frederiksberg, Copenhagen Business School Press.

Rio Tinto. (2006). "The Way We Buy: Our Statement of Procurement Practice." Retrieved August 29, 2011, from http://www.procurement.riotinto.com/ENG/supplierregistration/34_the_way_we_buy.asp.

Rio Tinto. (2009). "The Way We Work: Our Global Code of Business Conduct." Retrieved August 29, 2011, from http://www.procurement.riotinto.com/ENG/supplierregistration/34_the_way_we_work.asp.

Robeyns, I. (2005). "The Capability Approach: A Theoretical Survey." *Journal of Human Development* **6**(1): 93–117.

Sabherwal. (1999). "The Role of Trust in Outsourced IS Development Projects." *Communications of the ACM* **42**(2): 80–86.

Sahay, S., B. Nicholson, et al. (2003). *Global IT Outsourcing: Software Development across Borders,* Cambridge University Press.

Scheiber, N. (2004). As a Center for Outsourcing, India Could be Losing Its Edge. *New York Times.* New York.

Schön, D. A. (1983). *The Reflective Practitioner.* Jackson, TN, Basic Books Inc.

Sen, A. (1999). *Development as Freedom.* New York, Knopf.

Sinha, C. (2009). "Effects of Education and ICT Use on Gender Relations in Bhutan." *Information Technologies and International Development* **5**(3): 21–34.

Stainer, L. and S. Grey (2007). "The Ethical Landscape of Outsourcing Performance." *International Journal of Business Performance Management* 9(4): 453–469.

Steria (2011). *Registration Document 2010*, Group Steria SCA. Paris: 1–232.

Tencati, A. and L. Zsolnai (2009). "The Collaborative Enterprise." *Journal of Business Ethics* 85: 367–376.

The Co-operative Group (2011). *Building a Better Society: Annual Report and Accounts 2010*. Manchester UK: 1–180.

UN. (2008). "Overview of the UN Global Compact." Retrieved December 3, 2008, from www.unglobalcompact.org/aboutthegc.

UN. (2010). "UN Global Compact and Global Reporting Initiative Announce New Collaboration." Retrieved August 29, 2011, from http://www.globalreporting.org/newseventspress/pressresources/2010/elliott.htm.

Vilanova, M., J. M. Lozano, et al. (2009). "Exploring the Nature of the Relationship between CSR and Competitiveness." *Journal of Business Ethics* 87: 57–69.

Werther, W. B. and D. Chandler (2005). "Strategic Corporate Social Responsibility as Global Brand Insurance." *Business Horizons* 48: 317–324.

Willcocks, L., S. Cullen, et al. (2011). *The Outsourcing Enterprise from Cost Management to Collaborative Innovation*. Hampshire, Palgrave Macmillan.

Willcocks, L. and M. Lacity (2006). *Global Sourcing of Business and IT Services*. Hampshire UK, Palgrave MacMillan.

Willcocks, L. and M. Lacity (2009). *The Practice of Outsourcing: From ITO to BPO and Offshoring*. London, Palgrave.

Willis, A. (2003). "The Role of the Global Reporting Initiative's Sustainability Reporting Guidelines in the Social Screening of Investments." *Journal of Business Ethics* 43(3): 233–237.

Zadak, S. (2004). "The Path to Corporate Responsibility." *Harvard Business Review* 82(12): 125–132.

Index

DATE

MAY 1 4

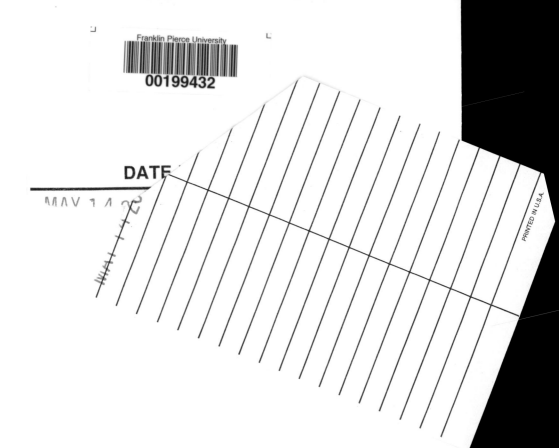

PRINTED IN U.S.A.